To Dr. Walter Judd
A foremost exponent
of A world under
God's Law

with warm regards —
Jean and Truman Davis

The World Under God's Law

Criminal Aspects of the Welfare State

by T. Robert Ingram

Rector of St. Thomas' Episcopal Church and School

Library Of Congress Catalog Card No. 62-16216

St. Thomas Press—1962

P.O. Box 35096

Houston 35, Texas

First Printing—1962

Second Printing—1963

PRINTED IN U.S.A.

FOREWORD

I have examined the advance manuscript of this book. It is the work of the author, as I did not essay to re-edit it in any way. From an early page in the manuscript I take the following:

> "The whole Christian doctrine of temporal government rests upon administration of a system of rewards and punishments according to the law of God. That is what we mean by the word justice."

Our hope of immortality is, according to the New Testament, a reward for righteous living, not by force but by choice. Looking further back to Joshua we hear him say, "Choose you this day whom you will serve." Still further back the ancient law giver tells his followers, in effect:

> "Let your laws be written upon the stones and the gateposts; let your priests proclaim them aloud; let the wives, the children and the servants hear. Obey these laws and you will be blessed in your stores, blessed in your basket and blessed in your going out and blessed in your coming in. And you shall be a great people among the nations of the earth. Disobey these laws and you will be cursed in your fields, cursed in your stores and your basket; you will be cursed in your going out and cursed in your coming in. You will be dispersed and scattered among the nations of the earth."

He gave them rules for correct living. They could obey; they could disobey. They were told their reward; they were told of the punishment. They had their choice. God never regimented or forced any man. The choice man makes is his own election.

The United States Constitution, influenced by the spirit of Christian civilization, breathes the same life upon us all. Jefferson, the author of the Declaration of Independence, proclaims the doctrine of choice and government by consent of the governed. With the responsibility of presidential office, he says to the nation: "Work out your own fortunes under a just government and an equal jurisprudence."

Justice Brandeis, an outstanding jurist, well said, "One of the unalienable rights of man is to be let alone." Not regimented or forced.

The author takes up in an analytical way each of the Ten Commandments, sacred to Jew and Gentile, and discusses its application to man. The author is not an extremist. He is an excellent minister, whom I have had the privilege of hearing personally from the pulpit. I have frequently read his sermons. He takes his text from the Holy Book. He interprets it according to the faith of the fathers. He is not intolerant, but takes the correct attitude of saying, as it were, "Every privilege that I claim for myself, I likewise accord to you."

In the interest of space we will only notice three of the Ten Commandments.

iii

First Commandment: "I am the Lord thy God; Thou shalt have no other gods before me." Exodus 20: 2-3

Referring to this the first of all commandments the author says:

". . . When the question of authority raises its head, all other questions retire to the background . . . No stable decisions can be made, no policies established, until it is known who will be the President."

The thought is that God alone is the true and only God. The temporal law is that proclaimed by the sovereignty of the land.

"Him only shalt thou serve. Worship is due no being other than God . . ."

When the communists rule a land God is set aside and the dictator allocates to himself all Godly attributes and prerogatives and the people serve him.

Murder is against the law of God as fixed by the Sixth Commandment. So is it said in the criminal laws of our state.

". . . God made us that way, and He gave us dominion. God's final act in the original six days of Creation was to make man, its crowning glory . . ."

"The dominion of mankind is maintained by preserving the dominion of every individual . . ."

". . . But if the dominion of man is to be maintained on earth, then individual men must avenge the death of any other man."

That is to say, man must make his laws and clothe his sovereignty with the power of avenging murder.

Every person shares the vengeance as a part of his own responsibility for the crime and for the vengeance. It is a solemn duty, a jury duty. The jury is our jury and it acts for us all.

Not only does Mr. Ingram call forth the parallel between the Eighth Commandment and the law of Christian nations calling for punishment for the crime of theft, but he goes further and calls attention to other acts, even by those in authority or those who would deprive the owner of his property by supposed legal process.

In line with the author's thesis we might well turn to Montgomery's history of a great nation, that of France, in which is written the following paragraph:

". . . peace prevailed; justice was impartially administered; industry flourished; the taxes were light; the towns practically possessed self-government; agriculture improved; . . .

iv

"But this age of prosperity was not to last . . . The small farms were one by one bought up by wealthy men, who converted them into extensive cattle and sheep pastures tended by a few slaves. Thus the independent peasant population was gradually driven off the land, and agriculture declined . . ." The Leading Facts of French History by D. H. Montgomery, page 14.

The historian continues:

"The law, in fact, regulated everything. A man could not set a price on his own goods; the government did it for him. These oppressions destroyed all public spirit and desire for life." Montgomery's History of France, page 16.

". . . God is not mocked . . . The law stands in all its rigorous purity, demanding vengeance for every desecration of man by any creature."

As against the collective theory of the communist, the author might well have quoted Christ himself: "Have I not the right to do as I will with mine own?"

Though the reader may not agree with Mr. Ingram in some of his statements, yet he must agree that he has shown a wonderful parallel between the laws of God and the temporal law of Christian nations.

WHITFIELD DAVIDSON
United States District Judge
Dallas, Texas

Pre-Lent, 1962

CONTENTS

Foreword iii

Punishment Vs. Regulation...................................... 1

What Shall I Do?.. 11

First Commandment 21

Second Commandment 31

Third Commandment 41

Fourth Commandment 51

Fifth Commandment 61

Sixth Commandment 71

Seventh Commandment 81

Eighth Commandment 91

Ninth Commandment 101

Tenth Commandment 111

Conclusion 121

PUNISHMENT VS. REGULATION

Whom the Lord loveth He punisheth.—Epistle to the HEBREWS

It is only as deserved or undeserved that a sentence can be just or unjust.—C. S. LEWIS

Thou, Lord, art merciful; for thou rewardest every man according to his work.—DAVID

Upon these two foundations, the law of nature and the law of revelation [to be found only in the Holy Scriptures], depend all human laws; that is to say, no human laws should be suffered to contradict these. Yet undoubtedly the revealed law is of infinitely more authenticity than that moral system, which is framed by ethical writers, and denominated the natural law.—WILLIAM BLACKSTONE.

1

KNOWLEDGE of God and of God's will is to be had from the Bible. The Bible is the record of God's particular interventions in human affairs, such as the Great Flood, the Exodus from Egypt, the Exile and Return of the Jews and the Redemption of the World by Jesus Christ. The particular intervention of God is to be considered in these pages in the giving of the Law. The Law is summarized in the Ten Commandments.

The liberal movement is dedicated to the establishment of a supreme world tyrant whose conscious human will is law and whose decree cannot be questioned. It cannot achieve its purpose until it succeeds in breaking down God's legal system built upon the Ten Commandments, and substituting therefor a system of regulation by law of all human conduct. The recognition of the Ten Commandments as law in the United States and all Christian nations is the bastion of defense of Christian freedom and a rock against which every tyrant must smash.

Let us first consider the purpose and role of law in general, holding to the simplest and plainest terms. I am, of course, considering law only as it is understood to apply to the workings of temporal government and not as the word applies to so-called laws of nature or science. I am talking about law as a co-ordinated system of laws which are written down, recognized and enforced by the ruling authorities of the various peoples.

We may ask the question, "What would you have to do first if you undertook to organize a new club?" Even among children the answer is forthcoming almost at once: "Set up some rules or by-laws." It is so essential and so elementary that we say it almost without thinking. It is the rules or the laws that mark out the structure or skeleton of any body of people. It is the legal system of any people which identifies a nation or an empire and locates its boundaries. That is not to say, of course, that a nation consists of its law, or that the law gives life and being to a nation. But it is to say that the law establishes a framework or bone structure in a people which gives them shape and individuality and form.

Law in its simplest form is the set of rules which are consented to and imposed upon all members of any group of people, and its purpose is to preserve the existence and identity of the group as a whole. The law sets forth the terms which every individual must observe for the sake of the whole body. The end and purpose of the law in this world is to protect society as a whole. The law protects the nation or the people from the vagaries of individuals. Punishment repairs a broken law; it does not protect or control. So-called international law restores order in the family of Christian nations after violations by a single government. Clearly the law giver in any case is the highest authority for any people. The origin of its law is its god. The final authority for our law is our God. Since we are a people under God's law, we are a people under God, or God's people.

3

Wherever the emperor is accepted as the source of law, the emperor is also hailed as god. If Der Führer or Il Duce, or The Leader, or the Soviet dictator, gives and enforces the law, he is openly declared to be god. If the final authority is claimed for parliament, parliament usurps the place of Divinity. Such a claim, in fact, incited a War of Independence in the American Colonies. But if the final authority is believed to be in the whole people, the *demos,* then the voice of the people is said to be the voice of god and we have set up the tyranny of the mob. So we who are a people whose god is the Father of Jesus Christ, the One who created all things and who redeemed the world, look to Him for our law. As a Christian nation in a Christian civilization, our law has its origins and its enforcement in the Creator himself. "Vengeance is mine; I will repay, saith the Lord."[1] Our laws are God's laws. We are a Christian people, despite the disclaimers of the liberals. In this connection I like to offer a statement from a prominent Jewish writer, George Sokolsky: "We speak of ours as a Christian civilization. But among us live some 50 races of man and some 250 religious groups, many of which are not Christian. And they should take no umbrage that we call ours a Christian civilization. Jews, Moslems, Buddhists, Confucians—all the non-Christians among us, realizing that men and women of good will respect their concepts of God and faith—must also recognize that in this year, 1951 years after the date accepted as the birth of Jesus, the great struggle is between God and the Devil, between Good and Evil, between Christianity and Marxism."

Ours is a Christian civilization. Ours is a Christian nation. Why? Because everyone in it is a Christian? Or even because its leading citizens are Christians? No indeed. We are a Christian people because the laws under which all must live—whether Jew, Moslem, Buddhist, Confucian, or Christian—are the laws which come from God and are enforced upon His authority through the mediation of Jesus Christ. Our laws, like all law, apply to every person alike, whether he be a Christian priest or an atheist revolutionary, a devout Jew or a Christ-hating Moslem. The laws are the conditions under which all men must live if they propose to remain within a society. They must be applied impersonally and with absolute justice. Their end is to protect society as a whole and to preserve its basic structure—a Christian republic.

There is a foreboding distortion of truth in the recent pronouncements from the Supreme Court of the United States to the effect that the function of law is to protect the individual from society. That perverted philosophy of law has produced a spate of decisions from the Supreme Court which are not only a travesty on law and justice, but an insult to humanity, an offense against nature, and a breeding ground of chaos and violence. It became necessary recently for the District Attorney of Los Angeles, William E. McKesson, to say publicly that this twisted and

[1] Romans 12:19.

4

inverted approach to the purpose of law was making it impossible for police officials to do their job. Said he, "Individual rights must give way when they transgress the rights of society." And again, "It is really society's rights that need protection. Society is hampered as long as its law enforcement officials can't perform their duties." Officers of the law, being subject to the law themselves, are not free to commit crimes either.

We are not to assume, as do our liberal wreckers, that individual rights are in conflict with the rights of society. I know of no rights which adhere to me as an individual which are in any way inhibited by the criminal and civil laws of the United States properly construed. St. Paul lists, in his vigorous style, the fruits of Christian life, which is not dependent upon the law, and then thunders, "Against such there is no law." No law can be passed against those things we do as individual Christians. Even we Christians have no liberty to commit crimes.

It is the God of Abraham, Isaac and Jacob, the God of Moses and the God of the Prophets of Israel, the Father of our Lord Jesus Christ, who gave our law. Christ confirmed the law God had decreed and fulfilled it. Christian nations recognize as enforceable by police and courts only those laws based upon the Ten Commandments. Oh, I know there are laws of convenience, like traffic codes. But even they have their ultimate rationale in the moral argument that lies in the Decalogue. It is that legal system which identifies ours as a Christian civilization and these United States as a Christian nation. It is a particular system; other systems are known and many prior to it. The Bible itself gives witness to many civilizations, laws of some of which have recently been dug up by archaeologists, that had law thousands of years before Moses. But when God made a Holy Nation, a chosen people, He did so by giving them His own system of law.

No other code of laws unfolds the tight moral argument of the Ten Commandments. No other code presents a thoroughly integrated system in which all the parts are bound together so that the loss of any one is fatal to the whole, or the complete observance of any one may be stretched to cover the complete observance of all. There is nothing like it anywhere else. And every people whose laws spring from the Ten Commandments become by virtue of that fact a Christian people. To live in a society where violations of these laws and these laws only constitute crime is to live in a society which is Christian. Clearly there are alternatives. Clearly there can be and have been nations and peoples whose god was not our God, whose laws are not our laws, and whose character and personality are not ours. For the first three hundred years of our Lord, Christian people stood with their backs to the wall against the immense pressures of the pagan world to impose upon them Roman law—law which had its origins not in God, but in the Vox Populi, later the Roman Senate, and finally in the person of the Emperor—all human wills. Roman law not only accepted

5

different origins for its law, but the particular laws it observed were quite different in character from ours. Adultery, thievery and the like were not major crimes, certainly not capital offenses; and the only real crime was an offense against the majesty and arbitrary power of S.P.Q.R.[2] The capital offenses under Roman law were political crimes—treason, defection, opposition, resistance. The savage penalty of crucifixion was reserved for political criminals. Julius Caesar startled the world when he let his political foes live. The death of Jesus was the death assigned to men who led political movements hostile to the authority of Caesar, even though Pilate said he could find no fault in Him. The crime posted on His cross was, "The King of the Jews." Barabbas, the prisoner who was released, is called a bandit, a word used in that day to identify the leader of an armed uprising against the state. In old Germanic laws and Anglo-Saxon law wergild, or man price, was a positive expiation even of murder: life could be purchased for cash, and the universal crime of murder, itself an offense against God's universal covenant with Noah, was reduced to delinquency.

A worldly or non-Christian philosophy of law is equally expressed by those people who say that the Supreme Court has spoken, and its voice is the law of the land. Whatever the government decrees, that we must do, say they. Christian governments have no such tyrannical license. They, rather, are limited in their power and can enforce only God's laws. All modern socialist states, which are established on the proposition that the Father of Jesus Christ is no longer God, have had to repeal the laws based upon the Ten Commandments and erect a tyrannous system whose only consistent thread is that nobody can challenge or question the power of the government. In Soviet Russia, we are told, there is no capital punishment.[3] There is no punishment at all. One is simply eliminated for crimes against "the people" (the Communist Party). In Russia men die for crimes against the state—but not for crimes against God.

The socialist system has reverted to the most degenerate of all the forms of ancient paganism, recalling Israel's bondage in Egpyt and the savagery of Carthage. The American flyer, Francis Powers, whose trial was a vast propaganda move to establish the socialist principle of human law, was not tried as a military agent of an enemy power but as a criminal. Spying was not treated as the act of war which it is, thus deserving whatever penalty the warring power deems fit, but as a crime. The meaning of that trial was that the world was informed of the new pattern of law to be imposed upon it: that crime is an offense against world government—not against God.

In the United States, where treason is defined as aiding and abetting an enemy in time of war, it has been next to impossible to imprison or

---

[2] "Senatus populusque Romanus"—referring to the public order.

[3] Some recent changes are reported that the death penalty may be inflicted in extreme instances, such as murdering a jailer.

6

execute anybody, except an out-and-out war-time spy, for treason. You and I cannot legally be put in jail for questioning the government, or disagreeing with its policies, except in its discharge of Godly law enforcement.

The alternative to God's law is not no law, but human law. Governments who do not jealously guard the majesty of God have no choice but to uphold the majesty of their own human authority. Where crime is not an offense against the moral order of God, it is an offense against the arbitrary power of the state. We were concerned earlier with a call to repentance, a call for men to turn away from the authority that pretends to stand without dependence upon Christ and to acknowledge Him as Lord of all things in Heaven and on earth and under the earth. We thereby recognize that men are normally in a state of sin, and that, in the power of Christ, we must make a conscious turning back to God in order to survive. There is another movement possible to men as shown in the Bible— the conscious turning away from God and back to the anti-Christ. That movement is called apostasy.

In the Old Testament the people of God who played him false were upbraided by the Prophets as adulterers. They gave themselves to other gods. They were more than adulterers, they were harlots who sold themselves, not into other marriages, but into wanton indulgences. The New Testament sees that there are no longer any other gods with whom a stiffnecked and rebellious people can dally: it speaks merely of "the falling away."

Christian people cannot turn from Christ to another god. There are none. None is offered in Judaism, or in Islam, or through Buddha, nor yet Confucius nor in the dark spirits of voodoo or the African jungle. Christians cannot play the harlot: we can only fall from the whole order of the supernatural and land with a crushing thump on earth. Satan, too, fell from Heaven to earth. He had dominion over the kingdoms of this world and his supreme power is the human power of death. Civilization will meet its death when the generality of men fall away from Christ and Christian law, and set up on earth a kingdom ruled only by conscious human will. St. Paul's description is classic: The day of Christ shall not come, he writes, "except there come a falling away first, and that man of sin be revealed, the son of perdition; who opposeth and exalteth himself above all that is called God, or that is worshipped; so that he as God sitteth in the temple of God, showing himself that he is God."[4]

St. John's vision is of a beast that springs out of the earth (not from Heaven), the ancient symbol of imperial tyrannical power. The beast "doeth great wonders, so that he maketh fire come down from heaven on earth in the sight of men." But his law is human and worldly. He causes "as many as would not worship the image of the beast" to be killed; and

---

[4] II Thess., 2: 3-4

7

"no man might buy or sell, save he had the mark, or the name of the beast, or the number of his name."[5] And the number of the beast is the number of a man.

There may have been times and places where these figures were obscure and dim. But this generation which has seen a half-mad paper hanger worshipped by a once great Christian people as God; and has heard its American President ask for billions to reach the moon in order to perform wonders in the battle for the minds of men; and has lived under a system of rationing where no man might buy or sell without a government card, can easily translate the curt words of the Apostles into worldly realities. The falling away is a matter of boasting in universities, and even among some clergymen who are quoted in popular magazine articles. The fall is precisely where John and Paul saw it must be—to earth. The new power must be that long ago foretold—conscious human will. The alternative to God's law must be the Apocalyptic horror of untrammeled human will insanely sitting in the temple of God where God ought to be. God ordains punishment for crimes against His law: the anti-Christ, a human power, kills those who do not worship him, or who buy and sell except under government regulation. Punishment under God is fair and just, God rewarding every man according to his work. Death under socialism comes merely for resisting the will of society: there is no punishment. There is no crime, only resistance.

Yet slowly but surely the legal system of Christian America is being weakened, the laws of God attacked, one by one, state by state. Already, in two of the states where this movement has gone the farthest, in Michigan and North Dakota, Americans can be put to death for treason but for nothing else. Michigan and North Dakota, strongholds of the new non-Christian order of society, boast no capital punishment, no death for crimes against God. But death for crimes against the state, for political offenses, is calmly accepted. Everywhere in the Christian world there is underway a powerful, highly organized movement to abolish the power of governments to punish men for violations of the Ten Commandments and to substitute therefor the power of the state to uphold arbitrary decrees, because say the socialists, when the government speaks it must be obeyed. If, they argue, we will submit to absolute human sovereignty, resistance to which must bring swift execution, men will have peace such as we cannot know under the moral laws of God.

The difference between a world under God's law and a world under human law may appear to be a subtle one and one with little consequence to everyday living. In the following chapters I shall undertake to examine the difference on a more familiar level—the level of particular laws under which most of us have lived. These laws and the system to which they

[5] Rev. 13: 13-ff.

8

belong are so ingrained in Christian civilization that most people probably take it for granted that no other system is even a possibility. Yet there is an alternative that is not only possible and foreseen in Holy Writ but has become an accepted reality in a vast part of the earth in our time and is steadily, like an advancing glacier, freezing large areas of American life. By considering each of the Ten Commandments in order, together with typical laws based upon each one, and then showing not only that each one is the target of a widespread organized attack for repeal, I hope to drive home the immediate and desperate implications for every person now living. It is clear that when a government ceases to enforce the Ten Commandments, it has no choice but to follow the pattern so clearly envisioned by St. John—to command worship of the imperial myth; to awe the populace with spectacular "wonders" of science, and to clamp all buying and selling in a vise of regulation and taxation. Such government controls of personal individual liberties describe all totalitarian or socialistic schemes. As we go through the Ten Commandments, the inevitable socialist alternative, subject only to conscious human will, will appear as an intended objective of those who so ardently oppose the modern criminal code. The laws fully controlling acts of worship through intricate management of the state system of schools are already drawn up; ultimately the penalty for violation of the school laws, at least for the possibility of the unbending objector, is death. The sky is already filled with zooming rockets, barrier-booming jets and whirling satellites. Control of the market has gone so far that even many of the old-line good-humored socialists are balking and trying to realign themselves as libertarians or devotees of the free market as a pattern for all society. These activities of governments are outlawed by the Ten Commandments: the two systems are contrary, one to the other. The result of repeal of each law of God is frightening to any sensible individual.

WHAT SHALL I DO?

Men govern by words.—DISRAELI

It is by virtue of the spoken word that men in combat gather courage.—COL. S. L. A. MARSHALL

Be ready always to give an answer to every man that asketh you a reason of the hope that is in you.—ST. PETER

A S GENERAL unrest spreads, and more and more people face up to the chaotic conditions being fostered by present lack of intellectual, political and religious leadership, it becomes ever more often necessary to answer the question, "What shall I do?" Scripture replies bluntly: "Repent." Literally the command is to turn back—to turn away from something and look once again to God. To each of us individually repentance has a particular reference. It also has a general application: that is, the corporate personality, the "state" in its full and proper sense of a collective reality, is called upon to turn away from reliance upon human power and to look back to God for guidance and leadership in public affairs. It is with reference to public policy that I propose in these pages to deal with some particular ways in which the generality can and must repent. Effective repentance also involves talking about it.

Surely it is plain that repentance is a two-edged sword, a double-headed eagle, as it were. I think repentance popularly calls to mind the bewailing of sins, undoubtedly because people who do repent do bewail their sins past. But such contrition is not at all a sufficient sign of true repentance. Many people are sincerely sorry for things they did that got them into trouble; but the reason they are sorry is that they have come a cropper. They are often like the child who is contrite, not because he got into a jam jar, but because he got caught. There are also the universal pangs of guilt. Few people fail to writhe and hurt under the stings of conscience. Even those who brag about their evil deeds, the ungodly whose mouths reacheth unto the heavens and who declare, "With our tongue will we prevail," even these people are acting out of a bravado that springs from a sense of guilt. One does not need to be a Christian to know that crime never pays, that the course of this world is tragic, and that we human beings are personally responsible for an unbearable amount of grief and violence. Neither does one have to be a Christian to regret sincerely all our wickedness. Yet being sorry in and of itself is not a sufficient sign of true repentance. True repentance begins from another direction; being sorry is a result of it, not the cause nor yet the fact itself. It is what happens to any person *after* he has repented.

Repentance begins with turning toward God. To turn to God means to accept my subordination to Him in all His ways, to acknowledge obedience and subservience to Him and Him only. The very instant in which I do so, I cannot help seeing clearly that my very act of turning means I have been previously looking elsewhere. I have sinned in having looked to other than God for providence. That is what sin means: it means thinking and acting independently of God. I have in some matter or other acknowledged an authority other than God. And no man can serve two masters. Surely I cannot realize I have been so openly guilty of such a gross sin as to make necessary a public turning to God without an overwhelming sense of shame and regret. Therefore, an immediate outgrowth of my repentance is a bewailing of my sins past; my repentance is not really my sorrow, but my joy at having at last put things right.

Today the people of our country are being stirred to the depths of our souls with anguish and pain over our admitted wickednesses toward God. There is no end of people who accuse themselves or others of this mistake and that one. Our liberal friends seem literally to wallow in guilt and shame, and are ill at ease if they can't find something about which to feel guilty. Our public affairs are clearly headed pell-mell toward disaster, from a government policy which supports our most vicious enemies, denounces our professing Christian friends, enslaves the respectable citizenry, and kowtows to the rabble. Violence is increasing apace and, despite the toning down of newspaper accounts, has risen to an alarming proportion. There is not only a frightening increase in the so-called crime rate, if we consider the actions normally handled by police and criminal courts, but we also have been confronted with organized mob violence in San Francisco, Jacksonville, Greenville, Madison, Ft. Lauderdale, Galveston, Juarez, and elsewhere, and with threats of violence by organized and obviously disciplined demonstrations in our own city of Houston.

In 1960 both candidates for the Presidency of the United States committed themselves to platforms of totalitarian pattern, and both publicly sought the support of voters whose aim is identical with that of the anti-Christ. There was not even an attempt on the part of either major party to apologize for rejecting the constitutional structure of our government and for repudiating the federal system by a deliberate usurpation of state police power.

I could go on listing the disasters looming ahead; no doubt most of you could do better than I. But to do so and no more, merely to shrink back at the prospect, is a far cry from repentance. To repent is to turn to God. General repentance means to acknowledge that God has both authority and cognizance over the so-called civil affairs of this and every other people. It is then to ask God, "What is it you require of government officials?" and, "What is it you require of the rest of us in obedience to them?" That is what the Founding Fathers did; it is what the general public required them to do. Let's not get sidetracked into asking whether Ben Franklin was a professing Christian. The point is, upon whose principles did he act? Did the Founders act upon the unchangeable requirements of God? Or did they turn elsewhere for their guidance? The answer is not even open to debate among competent students. It is beyond question that the principles of government upon which the various states and their union were founded were principles which assumed the Lordship of Jesus Christ. They don't make sense on any other basis.

Now some will say, Christians differ as to what these principles are.

I reply, such a statement is nothing but a confession of ignorance, or deceit. Besides, I am not about to ask you to decide between one principle and another; I am going to ask each of you to perform an act of repentance which consists of yourselves turning to God as the source of those principles, and agree we shall accept decisions that come from Him. We can exchange gifts of grace, and expect to find workable agreement. Let me cite a paragraph from the sermon of a colonial preacher, one Jonathan Mayhew, preaching in Boston in the year 1749, a whole generation before our War of Independence. " . . . it is proper for all who acknowledge the authority of Jesus Christ, and the inspiration of His apostles, to endeavor to understand what is in fact the doctrine which they have delivered concerning this matter (that is, temporal government). It is the duty of Christian magistrates to inform themselves what it is which their religion teaches concerning the nature and design of their office. And it is equally the duty of all Christian people to inform themselves what it is which their religion teaches concerning that subjection which they owe to the higher powers . . . "

It is your duty and mine to find out what Christ demands of us in temporal affairs. We are not concerned with the requirements of Democracy. If we do what we do because it is democratic, we are not doing it because it is Christian. It does not matter whether the thing at issue might come out in pretty much the same place either way; the point is that Democracy—however it may be defined—has been acknowledged as the ruling authority, not Christ. To turn to Christ, then, is to turn your back on Democracy.

The same goes for this world—this modern world. If we have been doing what we have been doing because of the demands of this modern world, to meet the terms and conditions of this world, we have not been doing it to meet the demands of Christ, or to meet the terms and conditions of Christ. True repentance, true turning to Christ, demands first of all that we find out what Christ requires of us in matters of temporal government.

Until we have made the search for ourselves and have some clear idea of what Christ requires, we have no possible way of knowing whether Christians do or do not disagree. People who are not themselves informed of what our religion teaches on the matter cannot possibly judge whether or not Christians disagree about it. Disagreement can be over many things. Husbands and wives can disagree. But it would be unnecessary to suppose they have disagreed about what constitutes a marriage, or what the Christian religion teaches about marriage, or even as to what the rights and duties of each may be.

I, for one, have given some years of study and thought to this question. I know enough to know I have a very great deal to learn. But I have already learned something which I offer simply as my own conviction as a result of my investigations: it is that the Christian religion, whether

15

expounded in the Roman Church, the Baptist, the Episcopalian, or what not, teaches fundamentally the same things about the rights and duties of Christian governments. Rules of reason and logic have a way of forcing all who would sincerely repent to a common course of action.

There is no end to the differences among us as to how far we are prepared to follow Christ; but there can be no honest doubt about where He commands us to go. The policies of King William the Conqueror and his Bishops were fundamentally no different from those of John Jay, one of the authors of our own form of government. Even the liberals or socialists who are so passionately trying to demolish these principles know perfectly well what it is they have set about to destroy. Remember the devils were among the first to recognize Jesus. And the enemies of Christ are among the best informed on the score of what Christian government looks like. The trouble with relying on a liberal scholar is that in his passion to destroy, he is apt to distort. Moreover, what the Christian approves, the liberal abhors. If you accept the liberal mind as the standard of approval, then you may hear the Christian position accurately described, but viewed with horror and alarm. For example, discrimination is said to be a bad word. It is simply wrong, say the liberals, to discriminate. Now Christians not only do discriminate, but we regard discrimination as of the essence of all Godly activity. Our whole life in Christ is a process of discriminating choices in every phase of activity—from acquiring knowledge to choosing our associates. We are told that it is an abomination to hold any person guilty by association. But Christians have always quipped, "Birds of a feather flock together." And Christian legal principles recognize the charge of being guilty as an accomplice to a crime by association under certain conditions with the criminal after the crime is all over. So it goes.

The socialist has no qualms about disagreeing with what Christ holds to be good, because he has rejected Christ's authority in the first place. But he is never in any real doubt as to what Christ has said, and what Christian authorities in all churches have generally agreed Christ said. I am afraid you and I are pitifully unprepared to enter into combat with these people simply because most of us have not bothered to find out what Christ says. Since we don't know what He says, we don't know whether people are in agreement or disagreement about it, and we are tossed to and fro from this moral judgment to that one without an anchor to hold to. In the following pages I shall set forth as best I know how what Christians have agreed are the rights and duties of both officials and subjects toward temporal government. I shall further show how these principles have been expressed in the form of government set up in the states of our land and in the union these states formed among themselves. And finally, I shall show that these Christian principles are under organized attack by the entire liberal and socialist movement.

16

The whole Christian doctrine of temporal government rests upon administration of a system of rewards and punishments according to laws of God. That is what we mean by justice. The execution of punishment is the specific work of the head of government. The cornerstone of the power or authority to punish is the power to execute the chief punishment, which is death. The death penalty thus becomes the symbol of temporal power in a Christian republic. The proposition is recognized from both sides of the issue, by those who believe it is good and right, and by those who believe it is wicked and wrong. John Locke, in his treatise on civil government, writes: "Political power, then, I take to be a right of making laws with penalties of death, and consequently all less penalties . . . and of employing the force of the community, in the execution of such laws . . ." *Consequently all less penalties* is the phrase that acknowledges the key importance of what is commonly called the "capital" or "chief" punishment. In the opposing camp, a Dr. John R. Silber of the University of Texas, writing in *The Texas Law Forum,* quotes Dr. Sheldon Glueck, of Harvard University, as follows: "The presence of the death penalty as *the keystone of our penal system* bedevils the administration of criminal justice all the way down the line and is *the stumbling block in the path of general reform* in the treatment of crime and criminals." (Italics mine).

The liberal movement confirms the key importance of capital punishment by its own dedication to its "abolition." It is necessary to try to strip the government of its power to kill in order to destroy Christian civilization and replace it with a reformed system whose head, himself, sits in the place of God and whose own will and decrees are the only things inviolable. The forces of the liberal movement all over the world began moving into position in 1958 for an assault on the power of Christian rulers to punish by death those who violate the moral laws of God. In 1960 the campaign swung into intensive preparation in Texas. Those in action there included primarily the Texas Council of Churches, the organized labor movement and the avowed liberal politicians. A headquarters was opened in Austin soon after the primary elections to seek the abolition of capital punishment at the next legislature. The same thing was going on in many other states of the Union, in England, Canada, Australia and, as far as I know, the rest of Christendom. You and I and our state governments are the targets of this mammoth drive. It is our way of life that is to be abolished. The reformed system would be a world government. There can be no world government as long as Texas, for example, retains its sovereignty. Texas loses what Christians have always recognized constitutes temporal sovereignty the minute it gives up the power to put criminals to death under the criminal code of God. The only alternative to utter chaos, then, is the identifying socialist passion to set up a government to rule the whole world. The socialist blue print for world government is well attested by a leading socialist spokesman, Dr. Martin Buber, who recognizes that such a government must be under man rather than under God. He writes that "for Utopia everything is subordinated to conscious human will, indeed we can characterize it outright as a picture of society designed as though there were no other factors at work than conscious human will."[1] And again, "if . . . the whole population is to be limitlessly determined in all branches of its life and thought by one central authoritarian will [God's will?], then it is inconceivable how such a stage can ever evolve into socialism."[2] Dr. Buber's willingness to subordinate everything to conscious human will while at the same time repudiating "one central authoritarian will" betrays a naivete inexcusable in a man of his learning and experience. Scripture not only foresees the passion for a world under man as a possibility to be realized in history, but forecasts its appearance in the rule of *one man* who is to be the anti-Christ.[3] The will of one man is the alternative to the will of one God, but one will there must be. The distinctive mark of a world government under man as opposed to the present arrangement under God is that it kills for political insubordination—rioting, rebellion, treason, spying and such like. Christian governments kill for insubordination to the Divine majesty—violations of the law of God.

It is fair to say that most Christians today have followed a long way down the path to utopia—the broad way through the wide gate that leads to destruction. The efforts to reform, or restructure the social order so that it will not be subject to the uncontrollable and arbitrary will of God but to the conscious will of man is a description of deep-dyed sin that has infected at least the articulate majority of the population of Christendom. Repentance will mean a deliberate turning away from the false dream of utopia, back to the reality of God in this present world and the hope of Heaven in the world to come. Repentance on a public scale will mean turning away from the drive toward a world under arbitrary human law and back to a world under God's law. Repentance will involve a careful re-examination of how the world operates under the law of God, which is law grounded on the Ten Commandments. Christian legalists, until the period of utopianism and revolutionism, took it for granted that law in Christian nations was valid only in so far as it was derived from and consistent with the Ten Commandments. In rejecting that common sense of our heritage, we have turned away from God. To repent will involve at least a return to a social order whose structure is ordered by the will of God, not man.

Christian initiative in repentance is the only defense I know against the immense, widespread, long time campaign on a public front to wheedle and coax all men into following the utopian, human, socialist line. It is people

[1] Buber, Martin, *Paths in Utopia*, Beacon Press, Boston, 1949, p. 8.
[2] Ibid, p. 89.
[3] II Thess. 2:3ff.

18

like you and me who are to be drawn away from our Lord, used as the instruments of defection, the betrayers and the deniers—the Judases and the Peters-in-the-courtyard. Some of us must see clearly and take responsibility for public proclamation of the Gospel of God's authority, not man's. It requires hard work to learn the truth, hard work to speak it out and hard work to listen carefully. Effort must be expended by all, some to preach and some to hear and all to talk whenever there is an ear.

It is an urgent Christian obligation to talk about these matters and to refuse to be bullied and silenced and driven into submissive isolation. While lack of information and clear understanding must be reckoned with and corrected as far as possible by each one of us, we must all realize that no one ever knows enough, or sees with perfect clarity, but that action must be undertaken anyway. Prior to action we must talk, and we must talk with the people we live next to, those we work beside and every individual with whom we deal. Talk is the first step of any action.

FIRST COMMANDMENT

I am the Lord thy God; thou shalt have no other gods before me.

THE first of the laws which God gave to Moses on Mount Sinai was this one. It is a reasonable first. In the establishment of a people, just as of a club, organization, or community, the question of who is to be the supreme authority must be settled first. When the question of authority raises its head, all other questions retire to the background. No more convincing illustration of this truth can be offered than the election of a President of the United States. The immense power and prestige of the United States government makes the matter not only of supreme domestic importance, but it is also an international event of a decisive weight. No stable decisions can be made, no policies established, until it is known who will be elected.

Important as the choice of a president may be, however, there is for all men a matter of still higher authority than the one represented here as the head of the executive branch of temporal or worldly government. That authority is the one than which there is no higher. It is the authority answerable only to itself. The name common among men for that supreme power or authority among them is "god." Religion, the force that binds men to each other as well as to god and makes a people, is first and last the question of authority self-sufficient, unchallengeable and supreme.

While you and I have been blessed to be born in a time and place where the knowledge of the Creator establishes Him as the only real God, we must recognize that other so-called gods do exist at his sufferance—things that are worshipped. The Bible speaks freely and unashamedly of other gods, not that God has real competitors, but that men do worship other powers as supreme. Moses was certainly neither so blind nor so stupid as to be persuaded that there was no god in Egypt, or in the Kingdom of Mari, or in the land of the Chaldees or in the cities of Palestine. The authority commonly recognized as inherent in these so-called gods was as real and present as in the Russian Politburo, the British Imperial machinery, or as is anticipated in the abomination called the United Nations. Then as now, many of the gods arrogated to themselves supreme authority and denied that they held their power at the sufferance of the Creator of all things, the God of Gods and King of Kings. So without any irreverence or disrespect or lack of appreciation and understanding, Moses could record God's own words which implicitly recognized the reality of such authorities among men as can properly be called petty gods. "Thou shalt have no other gods before me."

The difficulty disappears in the recognition of angels. These lesser powers are created by God who uses them to guide the destinies of nations and peoples. They know the true God and obey Him and worship Him. But one of them, the angel of light, the first created power, Lucifer, fell in pride. He thought to make himself independent of his Maker and to compete with his own Author. He is the arch-type of all rebels. The fallen

23

Lucifer is Satan, the spirit of the anti-Christ, the government which would arrogate to itself all power and bow before no other.

The modern word for such a government is totalitarian: a government that arrogates to itself total power. The crowning goal of Satan is to have a totalitarian world government. We who have known something of God the Creator know that total power can reside *only* in Him. Clearly the maker of anything is greater than anything he might make. The very possibility of a Frankenstein monster, the creation of human hands that can destroy humans and not be destroyed by them, is a false image of distorted reason. It presupposes a supernatural evil genius which deceives men into thinking they have made something while really they have been but passive agents of an unknown power. The potter can do what he will with his clay.

It is certain that the ultimate in supremacy, the greatest power there is, is the power to give existence to everything that is. God alone owes His own being to no other and has eternal existence in Himself. The mere possibility of total power residing anywhere forces us to recognize it in the Creator. Total power can be seated nowhere else. Any person who refuses to acknowledge that all things were made (and hence there is a Maker) simply rules out any consideration of the fact that total power exists anywhere. Thus, we may say that for both Christians and non-Christians there is no reasonable way to establish total power anywhere but in the Creator of all things. Apart from Him, all power is divided and thereby limited. God has not left Himself without witness even among the heathen.

The pretense to total power is the big lie, the hideous beast, the fiery dragon, the father of lies. For there is at least one power that ends any other power except God, and that is death. To cease to exist is to lose all power. Men, nations, civilizations, and even the sun and the moon and the stars, we know can cease to exist. Therefore, the power to destroy any is greater than any, save the power to make alive and to create out of death and nothing. When God gave man power over all the earth, He gave him the power to destroy anything in it, perhaps even to destroy the earth itself. But at least man has not only the capacity but the obligation to kill anything or any creature that presumes to kill a man, thus eliminating God's emissary. God spelled it out in His covenant with Noah. "And surely your blood of your lives will I require; at the hand of every beast will I require it, and at the hand of man; at the hand of every man's brother will I require the life of man."[1]

The creature, man, is supreme in all the earth, and government itself exists at his sufferance and rests in his hand. Yet man, although supreme among all things created, has not the power to override or ignore or disobey his Creator. Jesus, the perfect and sinless man, the Son of God who

---
[1] Gen. 9:5.

24

held power over all things, was tempted to think His was a power accountable only to Himself. Satan quoted Psalm 91 for Him—or misquoted it.
"It is written," said Satan, the arch rebel, "He shall give His angels charge
concerning thee: and in their hands they shall bear thee up, lest at any
time thou dash thy foot against a stone." The misquotation was "at any
time." Satan's reading would make it that Jesus, the perfect man, had a
blank check and could do anything at all, even to defying the order of
physical existence and jumping off the temple tower in safety. But the
Psalm does not say the angels will bear thee up at any time; rather, "in
all thy ways." As long as man proceeds according to the ways that pertain
to him, as long as the Christ engages in what is proper to Him, He cannot
fail. And so Jesus replies with the Scripture that pinpoints the way of man.
"It is written again, Thou shall not tempt the Lord thy God"—that is,
subject Him or lower Him to a proof of your own devising, forcing Him
to meet your terms. And He adds, "Thou shalt worship the Lord thy God
and him only shalt thou serve."[2]

"I am the Lord thy God: thou shalt have no other Gods before me."

Him only shalt thou serve. Worship is due no being other than God and,
therefore, to no creature whatsoever, not even to angels and certainly not
to heads of governments. For me to worship is for me to acknowledge my
own inferiority to the object I worship and, conversely, the superiority of
that object. The whole power of creation and preservation of the sun and
the moon and the stars and the governments of the world boils down to
expression in a simple act of worship by a human being.

Only the power who is to be worshipped can ordain the manner in
which he is to be worshipped. No man with an ounce of self respect would
participate in a form of worship which he did not recognize as itself being
authorized by the object of his worship. When Jesus instituted the Lord's
Supper, He plainly did so knowing that He was showing Himself as one
with the Father. "This do," said He, "in remembrance of me."[3] To participate in the manner of worship ordained by Jesus is to acknowledge Jesus
as one with God, Himself being worshipped as God.

Admittedly we can and do sometimes toy with the idea that it is possible to compel men to participate in the worship ordained by Jesus Christ
without usurping His place. Even the Apostles themselves clung to that
possibility up to the very moment the Risen Christ ascended into Heaven.
Christendom has tried it out many times. The scheme was tried of having
the kings and emperors of Europe compel conformity, or at least punish
non-conformity, at the direction of Popes and church officials; then it was
only a step to Popes themselves commanding Swiss guards as police and

---

[2] Matt. 4: 1-11.

[3] Luke 22: 19.

too well the horror that slowly oppressed Europe under that scheme until it exploded in the Reformation. The result was so conclusive that even the Counter-Reformation and the resulting doctrine of the Roman Church recognized the limitation upon the church to spiritual affairs. Otherwise the Pope would have sat in the place where God ought.

Luther proposed an alternative that the king could be head of the church. That solution was short lived indeed. Not only could Catholics not tolerate it, but many who rejected the Roman scheme also had to stand to the death against the Protestant scheme of king-bishop. The resisters were the spiritual and actual ancestors of these United States, men whose devotion and understanding were fired in at least 150 years of constant struggle and warfare in Europe and America. These men had watched their spiritual cousins drop by the wayside in compromise after compromise. They watched expectantly the Glorious Revolution under Cromwell, which stripped the Crown of its claim to authority over the forms of worship and the teaching of doctrine; but they also watched the heroic efforts dissolve in the fiasco of granting to Parliament what they denied to the king. In the reign of Charles II, Parliament passed the Conventicle Act of 1665 establishing and controlling religious worship.

Although those particular acts have been repealed in modern times, Parliament still regulates the worship of the Church of England and, despite the fact that a minority of its members are of the Church of England, has as recently as 1928 refused to change the English Book of Common Prayer. Parliament proved to be no more representative of individual human power to exercise consent to the manner of worship than the king. In spite of all the clamor about democracy, nobody has come up even with any machinery by which any man may delegate to the mob his own individual and personal consent to the worship he exercises.

At the time of the American Revolution and the adoption of the Constitution of the United States, men generally were sharply and bitterly aware of all this. Parliament (typical of all such governing bodies) was the last worldly authority that might be tried to represent properly the individual human being in matters of worship without itself replacing God. Now Parliament had failed. It had itself become the instrument of ungodly tyranny. It was with Parliament that our Founding Fathers had their quarrel. Shortly after the American Revolution a contemporary European statesman observed that it had been agreed in Parliament that, "The tax upon tea should be continued as a proof of the legitimate authority of Parliament..." From that hour it was clear that the ministry had no other object than to make the colonies feel their chains.[4] The bitterness of the long struggle with Parliament and the arrogation by Parliament to itself

---

[4] Gentz, Friedrich, *The French and American Revolutions Compared,* Henry Regnery Co., Chicago, 1959, p. 22.

of total power left its mark on the authors of the Constitution. The threat to liberty was for them neither Pope nor king, but the parliamentary bodies. From Paris Thomas Jefferson wrote to Madison, "The tyranny of the legislatures is the most formidable dread at present, and will be for many years."

It was thus under specific perils of the hour linked to decades of wrestling with basic principles that Massachusetts, Virginia, New York, and some other states wanted a Bill of Rights in the new Constitution to spell out their division of authorities. The First Amendment to the Constitution, the First Article of the so-called Bill of Rights, was the anchor. It offered the most sophisticated machinery yet devised by Christian men for pinning down the agencies of the temporal power and preventing them from encroaching upon the total power that can rest only in Jesus Christ. The First Amendment was, in fact, and is, a paraphrase of the First Commandment given to Moses.

"Congress shall make no law respecting an establishment of religion, or prohibiting the free exercise thereof."

"I am the Lord thy God; thou shalt have no other gods before me."

The basic law of the United States guarantees that Congress shall not usurp the authority over worship and by so doing put Congress in the place of God. It is to be noted that this amendment does not apply to any state government. It applies only to Congress and hits at the most immediate and present danger to the acknowledged Lordship of Christ. Parliament had taken control of religion and had virtually suffocated the Church of England. Our forefathers wanted no part of it. It is strange that today the elementary religious power of teaching the young should be one that this same government is attempting to usurp. It is also worthy of note that, as Jefferson saw, legislatures were merely the most immediate threat and not the only one. Today the powers of government are marching behind the Supreme Court seeking to snatch the authority of God by controlling the nation's schools, which have already been falsely subjected to state and local police powers.

The specific government arm has changed from the legislature to the court and the religious question at stake has been switched from attendance at church to attendance in school. The fundamental issue is the same as the one God struck at through Moses and through the Constitution.

"Thou shalt have no other gods before me."

"Congress shall make no law respecting an establishment of religion, or prohibiting the free exercise thereof"—such as forbidding Bible reading or religious instruction.

The First Amendment to the Constitution expresses what Christian Americans mean by the phrase, "separation of church and state." We mean that the state must keep its hands off the business of the church, which is the regulation of worship and learning. The principle is Biblical and imbedded in Christian tradition from the earliest times, even if often distorted and abused even as now. It is a principle by no means confined to the operation of the government in Washington, but is a universal truth held to apply to state and local governments as well. Despite the fact that many of the original colonies violated the principle by supporting established churches, and so did some of the states, there is no doubt that those responsible for the First Amendment to the Constitution were making a separation not between local and central government, but rather between spiritual and temporal authority. Neither is there any doubt that the issue was clearly drawn, and American tradition at least paid lip service to the universality of the Constitutional principle. James Madison dealt with the matter at length in connection with an attempt led by Patrick Henry to establish the Episcopal Church in Virginia. He left no doubt that the "separation" principle applied as much to Virginia as to Congress. Some of Madison's forthright statements as reprinted in the volume, "In God We Trust," by Norman Cousins, are worth quoting.

"The establishment proposed by the Bill is not requisite for the support of the Christian Religion. To say that it is, is a contradiction to the Christian religion itself; for every page of it disavows a dependence on the powers of this world; it is a contradiction to fact; for it is known that this Religion both existed and flourished, not only without the support of human laws, but in spite of every opposition from them."[5] In another line of argument Madison advanced the universal truth that human conscience cannot be controlled by civil government. "It is the duty of every man to render to the Creator such homage, and such only, as he believes to be acceptable to him."[6] And, finally, as I have stated herein, that "The Rulers who are guilty of such an encroachment upon the private responsibilities of worship, exceed the commission from which they derive their authority, and are Tyrants."[7] A tyrant then as now is defined by his usurpation of the place of God, by putting himself as a god before the Father of our Lord Jesus Christ.

The Constitutional principle had to apply to state and local civil authorities equally, and American tradition has so held. In its own weird usurpation of religious authority, the present Supreme Court has recognized that the doctrine of separation of church and state was intended to apply, and must apply, to the states as well as to the Congress, even though the Constitutional provision does not itself apply. The division is not a matter of degree, but of kind. It is not states' rights vs. federal power, but God vs. other gods.

---

[5] Cousins, Norman, *In God We Trust*, Harper and Bros., N. Y., 1958, p. 311.
[6] Ibid, p. 309.
[7] Ibid, p. 309.

It is precisely because the issue is not between local and federal civil governments, but rather a Christian foundation of all law for which all legitimate governments are administrators, that the complexities of enforcement in the United States have been developed. Not only do the several states police each other, as all Christian governments must; and not only does the Federal authority receive tacit support in its policing of the states; but also it has generally been recognized that the states have the obligation for policing the Congress. The long debates and actions over interposition and nullification hang on the intricate system of temporal authorities which were worked out to frustrate encroachment upon religious power.

The doctrine of interposition simply declares that the compacting sovereign states have an inherent responsibility to interpose their power between that of the central government and its people, if ever the central government violates the Constitution itself.

The South may have lost in the Civil War, but the means chosen to force a redress of what it believed to be a usurpation of authority was not only right, but the only means at hand. Many states outside the South on many occasions have been ready to go as far but have not gone to war only because they won their quarrels.

I am not advocating an armed attack by the State of Texas upon the government of the United States. I am merely pointing out that the basic law of the land, which forbids the worship of any gods other than the Father of Jesus Christ, has teeth in it. It has the same kind of teeth the Ten Commandments had behind them: the power to kill. When the Israelites in democratic procedure caused Aaron to make another god, Moses commanded the sons of Levi to slay the offenders. Upwards of 30,000 fell in one day. Man must uphold the authority and power of God by using physical force, if necessary, to prevent attributing total power to any other gods—whether it be Congress, the king or the courts, or all three put together. Moreover we, who deny total power and the attributes of God to our own Congress, would not be so base as to try to unite all power in the monstrosity, the hideous man-worshipping beast of the East River called the United Nations.

The attack of the liberal movement upon the Christian legal principle that the government should punish any attempt to establish a tyranny (an attempt to control worship by force of arms) is in the main a subtle propaganda campaign to turn the First Amendment upside down. Instead of being construed as an application of the First Commandment, the First Amendment is paraphrased as guaranteeing "freedom of religion;" that "freedom" in turn is interpreted to mean that the government acknowledges no God, no power beyond itself. There is no need to document this strange and erroneous interpretation because it is almost commonly consented to today. The state school system has worked well. An excellent illustration of how the Godless interpretation is applied, however, can be drawn from the many recent church-state decisions of the Supreme Court. There it is held that any practice in any institution connected with temporal government that acknowledges God, and especially Jesus Christ, is unconstitutional. There was a pitiful humor about a decision in 1961 upholding Sunday closing laws: the Court was at pains to explain that its decision had no religious grounds whatsoever, but was merely upholding the *humanitarian* powers of the state to decree a day of rest. Thus the Court expressly disavowed any intent to honor the Creator of the universe by a weekly commemoration of Creation; more particularly it disavowed any association with the only possible excuse for *Sunday* or *Lord's Day* closing, which is a commemoration of the Second Creation, the Resurrection of the Lord Jesus Christ.

The alacrity with which the liberal movement springs to the attack against any hint that the government might function under Christ is too familiar to need further illustration. It does need to be pointed out, however, that the very denial of a *Christian* basis for keeping the government out of the regulation or prohibition of practices of worship leaves only the alternative of a totalitarian *human* supreme will in the place where God ought to be. Apart from Christ, the principle becomes a legal guarantee of atheism. The government must be obeyed: and the government must forbid worship in any activities with which it is connected. The fact that this principle also results in a bald-faced violation of the Constitution against the prohibition of Christian worship is ignored. The fact remains that when the Court rules that the schools may not provide Christian teaching, it is prohibiting Christian worship. One may argue that the government has a perfect right to do so in *its* schools: yet it is the subjects of that government who are affected and whose freedom, unrestricted, to worship as Christ commands, is forbidden in a school they are required to attend. Two violations do not produce an affirmation: they merely result in confusion worse confounded. The attack is nevertheless pressed without letup.

SECOND COMMANDMENT

Thou shalt not make unto thee any graven image, or any likeness of any thing that is in heaven above, or that is in the earth beneath, or that is in the water under the earth; thou shalt not bow down thyself to them, nor serve them: for I the Lord thy God am a jealous God, visiting the iniquity of the fathers upon the children unto the third and fourth generation of them that hate me; and shewing mercy unto thousands of them that love me, and keep my commandments.

BOTH the Roman Catholic Church and the Lutheran Church today combine the commandment forbidding idolatry with the First Commandment, "Thou shalt have no other gods before me." As a result, they have to make a most awkward separation of what we regard as the *Tenth* Commandment, distinguishing between coveting your neighbor's wife and coveting his property. I think we of the Reformed tradition are fortunate to be familiar with our own arrangement because there is a very reasonable distinction between "idols" and "other gods." In the preceding chapter I showed that the other gods about whom we must be concerned are, as they ever have been, to be found in the seats of temporal, or human, government.

The Founding Fathers of the United States were keenly aware of the tendency among all men to raise their human leaders to positions of total power, making them gods. Our forefathers were resisting with their honor, their fortunes, and their lives the effort of the British Parliament to assume for itself total power, and thereby the power of God. They engraved in the First Amendment to the new Constitution the clause denying to Congress any voice in the administration of religious or spiritual affairs. "Congress shall make no law," they wrote, "concerning an establishment of religion, or prohibiting the free exercise thereof."

Idols are not, in this Reformed interpretation, "other gods." They are just idols. They are images and pictures. I have no doubt that idolators are also forced to worship "other gods" and to bow their necks to the yoke of totalitarian powers. But the peculiar activities associated with the worship of images are in a class by themselves. The words associated with the worship of other gods are "tyranny" and "slavery." The words associated with idolatry are "adultery" and "lasciviousness." The spirit of "other gods" is militarism, and its hierarchy or priesthood is a distorted control of legitimate force or the use of special bodies of toughs and thugs ranging all the way from Adolph Hitler's SS Troops to so-called racketeers. The spirit of idolatry is fornication, and its hierarchy is the dark underworld of vice—panders, prostitutes, and peddlers of pornography. The gambling underworld can probably be grouped with idolators, since gaming devices are also the work of men's hands.

The connection of idolatry with sexual lewdness is unquestionable. It is plain in one of the earliest accounts in Scripture. The children of Israel, tense and afraid as they plunged into the unknown wilderness of the Sinai Peninsula, panicked while Moses was away from them on the mountain with God. They came together and called for Aaron, Moses' brother. They quite democratically appealed to him, "Up, make us gods, which shall go before us."[1] Aaron obeyed the voice of the people. He gathered their jewels, melted them down, and with his own hands (or perhaps the hands

---
[1] Ex. 32:1.

33

of cunning workmen) cast and engraved a golden calf. When the calf was ready, the worship service was prepared and announced. Early in the morning they came to begin the business. They offered roast beef and barbecue and then sat down to eat and drink. When their bellies were full and their heads atingle with wine, they rose up to play. Their play was, as always on such occasions, a riotous orgy, a wild frenzy of debauchery, the noise of which came up to Moses on the mountain.

The Bible is succinct. But for those who are not satisfied with the Scriptural reference, there are available today recently discovered writings from the ancient world setting forth in disgusting detail all the unbelievably debased practices connected with idolatry. The Baals, so roundly denounced by the prophets, were the gods of nature worship and fertility cults. Their temples were houses of prostitution, and the groves and high places were scenes of reckless abandon. The rationale behind the connection is not hard to find. Any maker is certainly greater and more worthy than anything he makes. To worship the work of human hands, then, is in fact to worship the universal quality of humanity as maker. Aaron was petitioned to *"make us gods."* Graven images and pictures are the work of human hands and reflect the epitome of human creative ability. The creative work of human hands is the production of art in all its forms and supremely in graven images. We Christians know that to call human work "creative" is not to imply a power the same as the power of God, but merely a reflection of it. God creates all things out of nothing. Men can only make new arrangements of things that God has already created; and even their arrangements are only reflections and copies of what God has already arranged. At least that was the case until modern art, and I suppose nobody could tell what some modernistic compositions are images of. But let that pass. What we properly call creative work of man is in the realm of art and literature.

But there is one greater power given to man even than his artistic capabilities, a power inherent in nature and a step closer to the mysterious power of God to create out of nothing: that is the power of procreation—to beget children. To connect art and sex is to reach the peak of *human* creative power. So in cold logic the worship of the workmen's hands in recollection of procreation is an acknowledgment of the supreme creative power possessed by men—and we have a fertility cult.

There remains to consider the psychology of image worship. That, too, is evident. The image itself is under the control of its maker. But the worshipper must transfer the artistic ability of the craftsman to himself. Plainly, it is uninteresting for him to redesign his idol, or to paint it over, to try a more artistic piece of work. His human control over that image now leaps into the realm of images—our imagination. There, subject of course to the limitations of memory and will, the human self is supreme. The idol provides a stimulus to his imagination; the self calls up an imagined being in his mind who, of necessity, responds at once to every whim and wish. That creature of human imagination, called into operation by meditating on the image, is a sham and a delusion but seems to be almost a reality, and in the dream world effects a most titillating excitement. The dream figure may, for a little boy, be a superman, gun fighter, fist fighter, scholar, gentleman, or president; but for almost any adult he most generally becomes a perfectly agreeable subject to submit to his passions.

Anyone who wishes to read a masterpiece on the psychology of image worship should read the novel, *Descent Into Hell,* by the late Charles Williams. To be sure, any connection between the dream world and real persons is purely coincidental; but a stimulation of the imagination produces a real course of action, one that is directed toward a real person who can be hired to simulate conformity to the imagined personality. The movement has come full turn, and the temples of Baal and their prostitutes are in business.

I have gone into a description of idolatry at some length because I want to show that it is as virulent today as it was when Elijah overthrew and slew the prophets of Baal on Mount Carmel thousands of years ago. Furthermore, it is not carried on in secret groves by strange people in far away lands. I well remember during World War II that the immense respectability of *Time* magazine, though somewhat tarnished by *Life,* was given over to the encouragement of something called pin-up pictures, or, more euphemistically, cheesecake. Soldiers and sailors were supposed to require for their morale the stimulus of some photographic girlie images stuck up by their bunks. The character of all these recommended images made it plain what general tenor of thoughts were expected to flow from contemplation of them. Movies, vaudeville, radio, newspapers, and humor mongers joined the act, and I would venture to guess that pin-ups even invaded the rooms of home-bound married men and little boys. The atmosphere was so charged with all the lewd implications of these images and the only possible use to which they could be put that it is a wonder any military morale at all remained. In view of the notoriously deadly effect of such business on military morale, one cannot help wondering what sinister forces deliberately added fuel to the fires. Hannibal lost a war after his army wintered in debauchery; and that was long before the birth of Christ, in a campaign which no military man can afford to be ignorant of.

The full hot blast of the pin-up evil never hit me, however, until I came upon a captured Japanese trench on Peleliu. There, splattered under the blazing sun in the midst of blood and torn bodies, were the Japanese pin-ups still beckoning to the death of which they are the universal lure. All the titillating play of the imagination was gone now. But the filthy hags lay on the mud and gore still smiling. It all seemed to fit with the strange speaking, mysterious, heathen enemy. But suddenly it dawned on me that it was no different from what covered the bulkheads of forecastle and quarterdeck on my own ship where men were still alive. The same lewd idols infested our own Christian forces—and had official and public encouragement. I am altogether sure that General Lee, General Washington, Cromwell, Henry V, Louis of France, and Bernard of Clairvaux wept from Heaven as they saw Christian camps littered with idols.

Our experiences in World War II, together with the recurring public outcry against pornography in magazines and moving pictures—all highly sophisticated images—should be sufficient to establish that the practice of idolatry is with us today as widely as ever it was. I haven't seen much public ado about the vice underworld lately, but I have no doubt that it is flourishing. We all know prostitution is highly organized, national and even international in scope, aided and abetted by the traffic in narcotics, possessed of immense financial resources, exercising a network of political influence, and now openly linked with the international movement toward one world government. The last time I mentioned this subject in public it almost coincided with a detailed newspaper report from the FBI about a shipment of pornographic material prepared by Soviet agents in Poland and distributed through New Orleans to all the United States.

It would be a mistake, however, to suppose for a moment that idolatry begins with communism or flourishes chiefly because of Red support. It is just another unholy alliance in the vast network of organized evil striving toward total world rule. Idolatry is one of man's most ancient pieces of wickedness and demoralization. It is forbidden by law in every state in the Union. There are ample statutes against the distribution of pornography, the exhibition of lewd movies, or engaging in any activity associated with prostitution. Just as it is state government which must, in the end, put teeth into the First Amendment forbidding Congress to legislate about worship, so it is the local police and the state courts that must punish idolatry. It is absurd to expect police work by the Post Office Department's censoring the mails. The job is one for the local authorities. It is equally absurd to allow the United States Supreme Court to decide, when it permits *Lady Chatterly's Lover* to be imported into this country, that the book may also be displayed and sold in the local book stores without interference by police of the states whose business it is to deal with crime.

I have shown what idolatry is and how it is forbidden by criminal laws of Texas and the other states and other nations of Christendom. The Second Commandment is expressed in our own law today, just as solidly as the First. Now let me point to some organized attacks upon the laws dealing with idolatry which, if unchecked, would render those laws ineffective and probably remove them from the books and carry us one step further from a society in which crime is a moral offense against God to one in which the only crime is political.

There are a number of groups of liberal people who arrogate to themselves responsibility to preserve what they call civil liberties, such as freedom of the press and speech and religion. Prominent among these is the American Civil Liberties Union. There are even some left-wing legal aid societies that will furnish high-powered attorneys to represent people free whose supposed civil liberties seem to be threatened. Now I do not need to spell it out that one of these supposed "civil liberties" to be defended against a threatening social order is the liberty to indulge in pornography. That is presumably also bound up with a liberty called freedom of the press, or freedom to be an idolator, as the occasion demands. In other words, by the simple technique of invoking freedom of the press or freedom of religion, or, I suppose, freedom of speech, our liberal people lead the forces to guarantee the freedom to indulge in vice with impunity.

How ridiculous can we get? Freedom of the press means nothing more nor less than the freedom to differ with the government in print and not be punished. It was never intended to provide a vehicle for the untrammeled practice of vice. Freedom of religion means nothing more nor less than keeping Congress and the President and the courts out of the administration of church affairs and the work of teaching and worshipping. It was never intended as a cover to shelter practices of idolatry. Freedom of speech means nothing more nor less than that you can't be put in jail for speaking your mind about the government. It has nothing to do with granting permission to spread debauchery, lewdness, and evil abroad.

I have a friend, an Episcopal priest, who finds much to commend in himself in the fact that he blocked a group of citizens in his town who wanted to enforce their laws against pornography. He held out stoutly for something he called freedom of the press and declared that Christian people were expected to stride boldly into temptation and push their children into temptation, to learn the self-discipline of overcoming bawdy publications. It also had to do, he said, with separation of church and state. What nonsense! He was especially pleased with himself because the Roman Catholic Church was encouraging the militant citizens who wanted the police to punish purveyors of lewdness and idolatry and he thwarted a Catholic effort. Yet, it is an *Episcopal* prayer that asks the grace for temporal rulers to punish wickedness and vice. The propaganda of the Civil Liberties Union and its ilk, however, has been so effective that a priest of the Church thinks he is performing his highest duty in stopping the police from enforcing the law against idolatry.

There is another powerful assault being made on God's law by those commercial enterprises whose existence is attested by the filth they peddle. Just as the silversmiths in Ephesus stirred up a brannigan when Paul began to cut into their idolatrous market, so we may be sure the publishers of pornography, the producers of movies and plays, and the bawdy house operators are swift to denounce any Christian who raises his voice to enforce the law. I sometimes wonder if there is any lucrative publishing business at all aside from the junk that predominates on nearly all newstands. There isn't much else there. Even the so-called respectable magazines and playhouses specialize in titillating subjects, and the newspapers of Houston print daily appeals for the moving pictures which in themselves are disgustingly lascivious. Half of them seem to be covered with the teasing line, "for adults only." The illustrative art work is suggestive in the extreme; and the punch line is, "the most daring portrayal of intimacies ever shown on the screen." Whatever the films themselves portray, the advertisements that children read clearly presuppose that the reason most people have for going to a movie is to drool over a realistic image, in motion, of sex. People pour millions of dollars into the treasuries of the temples of Baal to pay for a steady flow of moving images to worship: the public moral atmosphere assumes that is a good thing to do. A commercial enterprise so far flung has to be highly organized and watchful to make sure the local laws of decency are not enforced—at least not any more than enough to get a little sensational free publicity.

It would be unreasonable and irresponsible not to assume that the modern "silversmiths of Ephesus," the men thriving upon a vast combine producing modern pornography in all its forms, would stir up a demonstration and exert all their power to avoid being put out of business. If they are quiet at the moment, it is because no serious threat has appeared. But just to be on the safe side, every so often someone comes out with a public proposal to "legalize" prostitution and gambling. Arguments are trotted out of the stable advocating government control of vice as being more effective than punishment for law breaking. Law abiding folk are thus kept off balance by an unthinking doubt on the matter, and they are inclined to be indulgent and look the other way.

Perhaps the most vicious attack on the Second Commandment is the one conducted by smiling do-gooders. They are so, so loath to keep anybody from doing whatever he wants. They see liberty as the absence of restraint. They are teaching in schools and churches, in psychiatrists' offices and doctors' rooms that people must be allowed to express themselves, that nature demands of us certain satisfactions, and that it is sex that makes a man a man. Restraints and self-controls are called inhibitions, and inhibitions are supposed to lead straight to madness or worse. The professionals are quick to exploit the theme. Not more than a couple of years ago one of the most widely advertised movies was based, according to the ads, on the theme that an understanding schoolmaster's wife made a man out of a bad school boy by introducing him to adulterous love. You didn't have

38

to see the film to get that story. It was displayed on billboards, in newspapers and magazines ad nauseam. Do you know what it costs to produce and advertise a film like that? I don't either, but it must run well into the millions of dollars. And it takes a big organization to spend a million dollars and then get it all back with profit. I call that idolatry with a vengeance, something to make the Ephesian silversmiths look like pikers and the Baal worshippers like Sunday School classes. The good-natured indulgence school even reaches into church literature.

There is the recent expose in Congress of the list of reading material approved by the National Council of Churches, which included books so obscene that the offending material was not even read aloud in the House of Representatives. Whatever may have been the explanation, it is an unshakable fact that the National Council of Churches gave religious sanction to the distribution of lascivious literature. If churchmen approve it, who can object? Fortunately, the Council of Churches is in no way representative of American Christianity, or any other, for that matter.

I have shown that prostitution and allied production, distribution and use of pornographic images, along with gambling, are crimes in the United States. The laws they violate are grounded upon the Second Commandment forbidding idolatry. These laws, however, are being neglected or actively opposed in favor of the theory that the government should arrogate to itself control of these activities and should not punish law breakers. In the wake of opposition to the laws or neglect of them has come a hideous wave of actual idolatry, representing a major industry organized in both political and criminal syndicates of a dank and smelly underworld. As is the case with all laws based on the Ten Commandments, if this one is not enforced, the alternative to enforcement is government control. Government control in turn means another area of human life subjected to the rule of man as opposed to that of God and another stride toward the socialist utopia which is a society organized as though there were no factors at work other than conscious human will.

THIRD COMMANDMENT

Thou shalt not take the name of the Lord thy God in vain; for the Lord will not hold him guiltless that taketh his name in vain.

ANY system of law requires certain basics to make it operative. One is a penalty for violations. Another, equally essential, is the inviolability of an oath. It is utterly impossible to administer justice, either in the punishment of wickedness and vice or the adjudication of civil disputes, unless men can be required to tell the truth on pain of heavy penalty. The requirement is met by an appeal to what men regard as sacred and inviolable. For Christians it means an appeal to God. To appeal is to call upon. To call upon the name of God is to take a solemn oath or to swear. To do that in anything but the utmost adherence to the full truth is to split asunder the whole structure of administration of law in all its forms.

To take the name of God in vain—to swear an empty or hollow oath, one that is false and meaningless—is to commit perjury. Perjury is a very serious crime. For example, although it was an open secret that Alger Hiss was betraying his government to the Communist Party, he could not be punished for that; he was, however, given a long prison term for perjury—for taking the name of God in vain. Originally, like all the other Ten Commandments, this one was intended in the Bible to carry with it the death penalty. Perjury is that serious—that deadly to the security of the social order and thereby to the lives of men.

Among the items of record preserved from the mysterious past before the Flood is the origin of swearing. It began in the second generation of the human race—with Adam's son, Seth. In the end of the fourth chapter of Genesis it is written: "And to Seth, to him also there was born a son; and he called his name Enos: then began men to call upon the name of the Lord."

In these pages we are talking about swearing and perjury in terms of legal proceedings and in crime and punishment. Yet I think we may well see in the matter something of far greater fundamental importance to human life than just the administration of law. Long before there is any record of the institution of punishment, men began to call upon the name of the Lord. Throughout the entire course of civilized history before the Flood, there is no indication that men had authority from God to inflict punishment. It was Noah with whom the covenant was made whose terms included that it was at the hand of man that God would require the blood of man. Still, men had long before recognized the solemnity and inviolability of an oath and, we may assume, found a way to manage their affairs by use of oaths. The importance of "taking the name of God" as a foundation of human society is indicated in the study by Jacques Ellul who writes that "the content of law is, in fact, fundamentally the same everywhere;"[1] and further recognizes the priority, even to criminal law, of law governing contracts and pledges which operate among all peoples and nations. The

[1] Ellul, Jacques, *The Theological Foundation of Law,* Doubleday, 1961, p. 28.

oath, "taking the name of God," is a pledge and the force behind a contract, which is only as good as the pledge of its maker. "Without a certain common concept of justice which recurs in all primitive systems of law, how can we account for such complex juridical phenomena as the contract and the pledge?"[2] The foundation for all legal procedure involving so-called civil disputes clearly is the Third Commandment, and it would certainly carry over its importance into the realm of criminal law.[3] Even today we find that oaths extend their force far beyond legal proceedings.

The gravest penalty for false swearing today is usually given for perjury in a court of justice. Sometimes we even run across the astonishing proposition that the only criminal perjury is that committed in a court trial. In 1960 the Texas Court of Criminal Appeals held in effect that a witness may lie to a legislative committee under oath and not be charged with perjury—only with false swearing. The difference is not apparent but the court distinguished in the seriousness of the crime, and the decision seems to have been intended not to uphold the sacredness of an oath, but to uphold the dignity of the courts. Why it should be less serious to take God's name in vain before the legislative arm of the government (or a private individual) than before the judicial, I cannot tell. But so the court held. Even so we may well admit that the conviction of a perjurer is a matter of some difficulty, and there is great difficulty in catching a person in an outright lie. So we find that the penalties imposed for perjury are quite often limited to offenses during a trial.

However, there are other important instances in which we today call officially upon the name of God in a solemn oath. There is the oath of office taken by every office holder, I am sure, in this country. Each one swears that he will do thus and so, "so help me God," often with his hand upon the Christian Bible. Every soldier and sailor in our armed forces swears in the name of God that he will do certain things. Witnesses appearing before legislative investigating committees are put under oath. And men not infrequently swear to their neighbors. Thus, to call upon the name of the Lord involves far more than just telling a lie on the witness stand in a criminal trial. The issue is not really the majesty of the court but the holiness of the oath.

It is significant that under some European Christian systems, a willful violation of a promissory oath is treated as perjury. We are assured in the code received by Moses that, whatever man may do in this regard, God will not hold him guiltless that taketh His name in vain. The Psalmist recognizes the fulfilling of even the unofficial oath to a neighbor as the

---

[2] Ibid, p. 30. It is unlikely that Ellul's main thesis is in accord with what is advanced in the present work.

[3] The early prominence of civil disputes over criminal action in matters of justice and judgment is shown in the recurrent Biblical warnings such as in Deut. 1:16-17: "Judge righteously between every man and his brother, and the stranger that is with him. Ye shall not respect persons in judgment; but ye shall hear the small as well as the great."

mark of a man walking in Godly ways in this world. "Who shall dwell in thy holy hill? . . . He that sweareth to his own hurt, and changeth not."[4]

Clearly the Scriptural view of swearing goes far beyond mere trial procedure; it raises the question of oaths such as are taken by men entering the ministry. Every deacon, priest and bishop must take most holy and solemn oaths. He is asked such questions as this: "Will you be diligent in Prayers, and in reading the Holy Scriptures, and in such studies as help to the knowledge of the same, laying aside the study of the world and the flesh?" And the answer is: "I will endeavor to do so, *the Lord being my helper*." That is calling upon the name of God under circumstances even more awesome than a criminal trial. And the Lord will not hold him guiltless that takes His name in vain. Neither does the church. To do so is to be guilty of heresy. The canons of our church, drawn from age-long Christian experience, provide for trial and defrocking of a clergyman who violates his ordination vows, or who holds and teaches publicly or privately and *advisedly* any doctrine contrary to that held by this church.

A heretic, then, is someone who teaches a doctrine contrary to the teaching of this church, which he has sworn to uphold, and does so *advisedly*. He is not simply wrong. He is wrong, and he knows he is wrong. But in all the horror of raging pride he declares, "It is right for me to be wrong." Although he professes by taking the name of God to believe in his heart the Gospel of Jesus Christ and to commit his whole life to the promoting of it, he will dare to say, as I have heard a man say from a pulpit in the Episcopal Church, "I do not preach the traditional Gospel because that Gospel is irrelevant to the modern world." He is a man who has sworn by all that is holy to spread the Gospel of Jesus Christ with all his strength. Now he says openly he won't do it. Even the Church, which can never punish, has always acted vigorously to purge herself of such wolves in sheep's clothing—men who have sworn to deceive their neighbors.

We may no longer turn heretics over to the government to be burned, but it is hard to see how they can be suffered to continue in Holy Orders.

There is still another aspect of calling upon the name of the Lord, namely, men can be required to swear. True, in this country, there is provision for those unusual religious sensitivities of certain peoples who understand they should never take any oath at all: they may, instead, make an affirmation. That is merely a play on words, however, recognizing that for such people even the "yes" and "no" has the self-imposed value of an oath before God.[5] We can be sure Jesus did not believe it was immoral to swear because He Himself did take a most solemn oath. During His trial before the council the high priest administered the oath and demanded an

---

[4] Psalm 15.

[5] Certain Christians, taking the teachings of Jesus with utmost seriousness, understand that He forbade all oaths when He said to swear not at all, but let your yea be yea and your nay, nay. Generally, however, this teaching is understood to be, not that it is wrong to swear, but that our tongues should be so guarded that every word we utter has the sacredness of an oath.

45

answer—which he got. "I adjure thee by the living God," he cried to Jesus, "that thou tell us whether thou be the Christ the Son of God." Jesus answered him, "Thou hast said." (An idiomatic "yes").[6] We have, therefore, no good reason for supposing oaths are forbidden—only that their sacredness and inviolability may even extend to every word a Christian speaks. Thus even a lie, for a Christian, is taking God's name in vain, for he has sworn that his whole life is in, of, by and for God.

With all this in view, it is indeed strange that so much Christian teaching about the Ten Commandments does not even treat the Third Commandment as a prohibition against perjury, heresy and lying, but as a sort of good mannered objection to coarse or vulgar language. I certainly do not recommend the use of vile language. But there is no Divine law against it. Neither should this commandment be used to restrict the familiar use of God's name in every day speech—God bless you, or good-bye (God-be-with-you), or the Swiss greeting, Praise God. Nor should it be held up as a law against cursing. Certainly Christian people do not utter curses lightly. Yet again, Jesus pronounced terrible woes on some men. The utterance of a curse is terrible but not against the law.

It is a crime, however, to take God's name in vain. Under the laws of Texas it is a most serious crime. And in many Christian systems even willful violation of a promissory oath, such as heresy, is punishable, sometimes by death.

There is a significant corollary to oath taking. It establishes legal recognition of God. Whoever it is by whom men swear is the law's god. In the United States He is plainly the Father of Jesus Christ. While the Constitution of the United States may forbid sectarian religious tests for holding federal office, every president, every congressman and senator and most other officials must swear by God. To do so is to acknowledge the Creator and that He is God.

Now let us consider how the laws to punish all who take the name of God in vain are under attack, and what alternative is being proposed. We may well look first to the prevailing religious attitude toward the matter, especially as it affects the particularly religious concern of heresy. It has been years since there has been a heresy trial in the Episcopal Church, and only a handful have been conducted in the United States in any church outside the Roman Church in the last half century. Behind that testimony of silence lies the organized mockery and scorn that has been heaped upon those who would strive to drive out false doctrine. In the spirit of our times it is supposed to be positively immoral, intolerant if you please, to proceed against someone who advisedly falsifies the teaching he has sworn to uphold. Nonetheless, one of the oaths taken by every priest, who certainly would not fail to quake before the law of the God

---

[6] Matt. 26:63-64.

46

he proposes to serve, reads as follows: "Will you be ready, with all faithful diligence, to banish and drive away from the Church all erroneous and strange doctrines contrary to God's Word; and to use both public and private monitions and exhortations, as well to the sick as to the whole, within your Cures, as need shall require, and occasion shall be given?" The response is, "I will, the Lord being my helper."

We must see then, either that little or no false and erroneous doctrine is in the churches, or that some deacons, priests and bishops have ignored this oath and have taken the name of the Lord our God in vain. In the light of certain public writings and utterances of James A. Pike, Episcopalian Bishop of California; and of the endorsement that functionary has received from other bishops and priests; and of the article in a magazine of immense national circulation to the effect that some 40 per cent of the young ministers involved in a survey declared they did not believe the fundamental doctrines of the faith they were sworn to propagate,[7] there is little doubt the law is being flaunted. There must be literally thousands of clergymen in the United States who have themselves taken God's name in vain with impunity, either in swearing falsely about what they would teach and preach, or in swearing falsely that they would "be ready, with all faithful diligence, to banish and drive away from the Church all erroneous and strange doctrines contrary to God's Word." It would seem fair to conclude without even further examination that these men are making a mockery of oaths and so are attacking God's law at its roots.

The airy unconcern with which the present generation of clergy reacts to vain swearing attacks the sacredness of all oaths at the root. Small wonder that civil authorities are less and less vigilant in enforcing oaths. In the nature of the thing we would not expect to find any concerted action openly supporting the practice of perjury. Rather we would expect to find a steady eating away at anything giving public and legal force to the sacredness of the name of God. The only evidence that such eating away is part of an organized effort would be in the scale on which it occurs, the similarity of approach and the persistence of action beyond any reasonable expectation of purely irrational sinfulness. Since it is a matter of common knowledge that the entire socialist movement is an organized plan to wipe the slate of history clean and destroy all existing public order (status quo), in order to prepare the earth for a new society subject only to conscious human will, it would be surprising indeed if socialist groups everywhere were not busily engaged in eliminating the oath. Socialist scorn for swearing is as much a matter of common knowledge as the socialist objective. Only a few instances need be mentioned. The World Court, for example, presumably the new fountain of justice, or a prototype of the socialist dream of world government, has no provision

---

[7] *Redbook*, October, 1961.

for "taking the name of God"—no oath. Left wingers evidence a policy of refusing to swear before a legislative committee by "taking the Fifth Amendment." Under that procedure the oath, which Jesus Himself accepted from the High Priest at His trial, a foundation of ordered human life, is made secondary to a vague ideal called the Fifth Amendment, which merely recognizes that the witness of any man either for or against himself is not sufficient.[8] Lenin's famous dictum accurately describes the Soviet Socialist attitude toward an oath as represented in a treaty: for him it is like a pie—useful to be cut up and divided according to the exigencies of the moment.

Perhaps more alarming and more to the point is a 1961 decision of the Supreme Court, admittedly socialistic in bias, which overruled a provision of the Maryland Constitution which seems to make "a declaration of belief in the existence of God" mandatory for holding "any office of profit or trust in this state." The case was *Torcaso vs. Watkins.* The grounds for the action was the objection of one Roy R. Torcaso to that provision as it applied to himself, an avowed atheist, in taking office as notary public. He was refused his commission for this office, by the clerk of the circuit court, because he would not subscribe to an oath involving a declaration of belief "in the existence of God." Felix Morley, in *Nation's Business,*[9] shrewdly points out "the absurdity of having an official administer to others oaths in the sanctity of which he does not himself believe." The absurdity seems to be quite as irrelevant to the court as the sanctity of the name of God. So the Supreme Court ruled it is more important to sanction atheism and overruled the Maryland Constitution. The effect is not only to eat away further at the sacredness of the name of God, but also to eliminate the oath itself. These few random illustrations are sufficient to show beyond a reasonable doubt that a broad, organized attack reaching into high places is under way to remove the Third Commandment from legal standing in the United States and throughout the world.

Not only is this attack evident from widespread actions, but also from the admitted philosophical base upon which socialism seeks to justify itself. That base is commonly recognized to be in the work of the Prussian scholar, George Wilhelm Friedrich Hegel. Hegel was the apologist for the innovation of the Prussian "paternalistic" state—the full-blown prototype of all modern totalitarian systems. The sum of Hegel's tortured reasonings is simply, "The state is God walking upon earth." With that thesis, Hegel threw wide the gates of Hell from which has continued to emerge the proposed structure of government over which at the end the anti-Christ of the New Testament is expected to rule. The head of such a state, when it at last achieves world dominon, sits where God ought. He will be *the* anti-Christ. Under the Hegelian concept there is no room

[8] See John, Chapter 5.
[9] September, 1961.

48

for "taking God's name," no sense in an oath. The state is in no way dependent upon the reliability of pledges and contracts: in fact, it refuses to recognize their validity. Only the state has a cause: before it, individuals' claims and powers fade away. There is no occasion for judging between a man and his brother. They need only to submit to government control and all, presumably, will be well.

FOURTH COMMANDMENT

Remember the Sabbath Day to keep it holy. Six days shalt thou labour, and do all thy work: but the seventh day is the Sabbath of the Lord thy God: in it thou shalt not do any work, thou, nor thy son, nor thy daughter, thy manservant, nor thy maidservant, nor thy cattle, nor thy stranger that is within thy gates: for in six days the Lord made heaven and earth, the sea, and all that in them is, and rested the seventh day: wherefore the Lord blessed the Sabbath Day, and hallowed it.

THE Sabbath law would seem to be straightforward enough. It establishes a legal holy day commemorating Creation, during which work is suspended; it is so comprehensive in its scope as to leave no loopholes. It specifically includes slaves and foreigners, and even domestic animals. The suspension of work is universal. It is equally clear that, like all holy days, this one is a commemoration of an historical event. The Sabbath Day commemorates in awesome solemnity the original Creation of all things that exist whether in Heaven or upon earth. We need not here get into the question of how long it took God to finish *His* Creation, or what the Bible actually says about it, or what we are to do with the speculations of modern gnostics about evolution. It is certainly admitted on all sides that the Bible begins and ends upon the assumption that God created every thing: it cannot be squared with the assumption that He didn't—that all things evolved in a self-creating process. It must also be admitted that, however long a period of time God may have taken to do his creating, He is assumed by all Biblical writers to have finished it. It is further assumed that He worked in six stages—whether we call them days or eras or epochs is immaterial. There were six closed periods. When the whole thing was done, God saw that it was very good; and He rested.

I have no information as to whether the civilized world before the time of Moses had a seven-day-week or a weekly holy day commemorating the original Creation. But there is no doubt that, when God gave His law to Moses to organize the People of God, He ordained the seventh day in recurring cycles of weeks to be a legal holiday celebrating the Creation. It was to be observed, like all legal holidays, by a cessation of the normal routine of work, enforced by law. The rhythm of the Sabbath imposes upon time a character independent of the moon and the seasons. It is utterly dependent upon the obedient will of man imposed through the machinery of law. There is nothing about this day in nature to distinguish it from any other day—a Wednesday or a Friday or anything else. It is set apart and characterized completely by law which is voiced, written and enforced through human activity. The week itself is established by the Sabbath law.

The importance of the week in human affairs has been correctly gauged by many great men. Ralph Waldo Emerson, the New England transcendentalist, is quoted somewhere as saying: "The core of civilization is the Sabbath." Its importance is equally measured by the enemies of God and of civilization. Foremost among these must be counted Francois de Voltaire, a French thinker whose ideas played a dominant part in the atheistic French Revolution. Voltaire is credited with saying, "If we want to destroy the Christian religion, (which he did) we must destroy the Christian sabbath." The anti-Christian regime set up in France by the Revolution attempted just that: to destroy the Christian Sabbath as part of the cam-

53

paign to wipe out both the Christian faith and the civilization which rested on it. The Revolutionary government, looking glassy-eyed at the decimal system, tried to institute a ten-day week, a cycle of time celebrating the mathematical genius of mankind as the goddess of reason, and to eliminate the commemoration of the Creator. The Communist regime of Soviet Russia made a similar attempt in 1917, I am told.

It is recognized by both the Godly and the ungodly that the institution of the Sabbath is a willful and arbitrary cycle of time which exists to honor the Creator. To see that is to see the absurdity of two popular explanations of the Sabbath, both of which unfortunately are spread by unthinking clergymen as well as by deliberate enemies of God and Christ. The first is that the story of Creation was written to explain why the week was a cycle of time. The second is the work of the self-styled "benefactors," or do-gooders, of whom Jesus took note: they say it was instituted as an act of humanitarian wisdom and public hygiene. The error of the first group is one that carries the battle flag of the Devil. It puts everything backwards and upside down: it does all it can in reverse, calling good evil and seeing evil as good. The connection between the Sabbath and the story of Creation is obvious. But it is equally obvious that unless the story is to be seen as a falsehood and a myth, the event came first and the Sabbath later. The fact that the observance of the Sabbath rests upon legal enforcement rather than by observation of the motion of the elements should be sufficient to establish the Christian view. It is an arbitrary form for commemorating a unique event. The Christian view should be supported by the conviction of various anti-Christians that it can be changed by law quite as effectively as it can be established by law. Any argument that the seven-day-cycle has a mystical bond with nature and laws of health and hygiene is easily exploded by the fact that pagan civilization thrived for hundreds of years without a Sabbath.

The second false popular explanation is more subtle. It is expounded in a recent book on the Ten Commandments by an English clergyman, H. G. G. Herklots.[1] (Incidentally, Mr. Herklots recognizes that interest in the Ten Commandments is so low at the moment among thinkers that nothing of importance on the subject has appeared in print until now for some half a century or more). Mr. Herklots, however, does not deal with the Sabbath as a holiday established to commemorate the miracle of Creation: he says it was the product of humanitarianism among the Jews who wanted to let their mules and their slaves have a day off. Clearly Mr. Herklots grew up during the madness of the welfare state. The clarity of his thinking is questionable, moreover, by his astonishing leap of logic from the legal Sabbath to an argument for integration of the races. I cannot find any reasonableness or shadow of truth in either the idea that

---

[1] Herklots, H. G. G., *The Ten Commandments and Modern Man,* Essential Books, Inc., Fairlawn, N. Y., 1958.

the Creation story was written to explain the legal seven-day-week or that its aim was humanitarian sentimentalism. I find the reasonableness of the Biblical account and Christian interpretation overwhelming. The Sabbath is an institution established in law to commemorate the original and great miracle of all time—Creation. Only that interpretation can be allowed if we are to agree that Christian people, although not ruled by law, do observe the law. For the Christian weekly holy day is not the Sabbath, or Saturday, but the Lord's Day or Sunday, the first day of each week. At least that is true among us who are heirs of Gentile Christianity, not of Jewish.

The Jewish Christian in the first century continued to observe the law, keeping Saturday zealously, and then adding Sunday worship in Christ. It was agreed all around, however, that the Gentiles, who had never had the law, could not be put under its yoke in Christ and need not be circumcised and join the Jewish community in order to become Christian. It is unnecessary further because the observance of the Lord's Day, or the first day of the week as holy, implies recognition of what is involved in the Sabbath. As with all things Christian, life in Christ presupposes and absorbs into itself all other Godly requirements. The observance of the first day of the week, which is properly called the Lord's Day, is a commemoration of His resurrection from the dead. When Jesus stepped alive and in His glorified body out of the tomb, He was the first of a new creation. The significance of that mighty act was universally recognized by Christians. We who are in Christ are what St. Paul calls a new creature. Christ is the second Adam. Jesus spoke of a second birth. The Church Fathers, men who piloted the Christian Community through the first centuries of building up, spoke often of the Second Creation. The whole work of Christ may be summed up as the work of a second creation, and the darkness that covered the earth on Good Friday was foreshadowed in the darkness that covered the deep in the beginning. Now there can be no second birth, no second creation, unless there was a first. To observe what we openly commemorate as the new act of creation is to declare that we recognize and reverence the first.

It is for this reason that Christian people often do not celebrate their natural birthdays, but rather their date of baptism: families often commemorate the anniversary of death, even, instead of birth, as the beginning of immortal life. In either case, commemoration of the second takes up into itself the first: observance of the first does not imply the second. The Christian observance of the Lord's Day also implies and reconfirms the seven-day-week set up legally by the Sabbath to honor God's mighty act of Creation. The Lord's Day is the first day of the week—a day which would not be the first day unless there were a seven-day-week in commemoration of the original Creation. The Lord's Day is an intrusion of eternity into time since it is not only the first day, established in and on time, but is also the eighth day. Christians speak of the octave or eight-day cycle which introduces into time a foretaste of everlasting life. The octave is expressed in the Christian scale of music which has, uniquely, seven notes. The eighth note of the scale—octave—is the first and the last. It also figures eternity for us. For high C, the octave of low C, is the same note but an octave higher and different, beginning a new cycle of notes each one an octave higher. When the scale is carried on up, it runs into sounds beyond the human ear and advances into new realms of being. So the establishment of the week to commemorate the Creation is reaffirmed in Christ.

Of course, I know it is possible for some liberal scholar to maintain that some sinister, ecclesiastical, power-hungry, evil geniuses made up the whole Gospel account in order to reconstitute a holy day other than the Sabbath. But I don't think anybody who is capable of reasonable thought will take it seriously. As for any humanitarian by-product of the Sabbath observance, it is as well accounted for by the Lord's Day observance as by the Sabbath, or Saturday, closing. The cycle of rest is still one day in seven, and even the benefactors, or do-gooders, can rest as happy on Sunday as ever before. I don't know what we can do about those militant benefactors who now want two days of rest, or even three and four. Perhaps they can improve upon Christ and, without doing away with the seven-day commemoration of Creation, impose upon it a two- or three-day enforced rest in commemoration of human laziness. But at least we who are Christian can rejoice in the glorious mystery of the Lord's Day observance, enforced by law, which commemorates both the second and first creative acts of God and gives to man both rhythmic rest and a framework of civilized order, a foretaste of the rest in eternal activity in God.

Common knowledge should confirm the thesis that this commandment is carried in the laws of the several states and other Christian states and enforced by them. Every so often a newspaper feature surveys the field. Usually such an article, like one carried by the Associated Press for Sunday papers during a nation-wide anti-Sabbath drive of 1960, lampoons the laws and attempts to dig up examples that seem to border on the ridiculous.[2] Despite the ill will, however, such articles serve admirably to demonstrate the universality of Sabbath laws. The existence, universally, of Sunday closing laws is admitted by decrying them. They are not called Sabbath regulations or even Lord's Day rules, but blue laws. Furthermore, although people generally have no idea of the turmoil going on all around because of these laws, such articles report it exists. This reporter says so. Most people thought last Sunday was a peaceful day. But, says the reporter, not so. Its peace was "shattered by arguments" and hog-tied by a "maze

---

[2] Associated Press for Sunday papers, October 16, 1960.

of laws more tangled than a spider web in a hurricane." See what a turmoil most people missed?

Really it is quite immaterial that the laws of Texas are vastly different from those of New Jersey or Virginia. I do not find my worship in any way interfered with by the fact that some of these laws make us laugh because they are no longer relevant: such as forbidding miniature golf. But mockery has ever been the work of the Devil, and one way to attack the Ten Commandments is to interpret them as absurdity. The whole Bible is attacked that way, for that matter. You know, really, nobody-who-is-anybody-anymore-would-take-that-seriously sort of thing.

But reading on past the mockery in the article referred to, it is established there by our foes that Sabbath laws are part of the American legal structure. The fact that they vary only confirms the real nature of legal observance: it is impossible to make any day holy by law. Jesus showed that clearly. Nevertheless, the law must impose regulations; and the mere fact that there are regulations establishes a legal holiday. It really doesn't matter whether it is miniature golf that is outlawed on Sunday or selling beer over the bar. The point is that the day is different from every other day, and the law is set up to enforce that difference by whatever particulars a local community decides upon. Certain matters are accepted as symbols of public rest: as long as those symbols are protected by law the Sabbath is secure, or the Lord's Day is a legal holiday. There is no need for a policeman in every house.

The occasion for this particular bit of syndicated sneering was the fact that the Supreme Court of the United States, which constitutionally has no jurisdiction over such internal state affairs, had agreed to decide whether the Constitution allows the states to have these laws which they have had from their inception. Behind this suit lies a fascinating and intricate pattern of organized maneuver. About the same time Houston was confronted with three chain grocery stores announcing they would stay open on Sunday, the same kind of thing was going on from North Carolina to California. The AP says Sunday closing laws were then at issue in seventeen states. All at once Americans in seventeen states became concerned about Sunday closing laws—or blue laws if you prefer. It is one of those coincidences like the demonstration that burst out spontaneously all the same day among our soldiers from Singapore to Berlin to go home after the war. (In Honolulu every leader of the so-called spontaneous demonstrations was found to be a long-identified Communist party worker. But I am sure they, too, were moved by spontaneity.) In any event, in seventeen of the United States, some chain grocers suddenly found all at the same time that they couldn't supply a community with groceries in six days and had to have seven. In several of these states Christian people, in shocked surprise, insisted that the laws they had must be enforced. Enforcement brought the next phase of the campaign in that suits were filed in three states challenging constitutionality of these laws. They were in Pennsylvania, New Jersey and Maryland.

We may be sure that out of the crop of enforcements in seventeen states, the attackers picked those that best suited their long range purpose. The purpose is plainly stated: to declare all Sunday closing laws unconstitutional. Now notice what that means. It means simply that no state can declare a legal holiday whose purpose is to honor the Creator by commemorating the second or first creations. Presumably there is no objection to any regulations to declare holidays and enforce them for other purposes: say, Mother's Day, or May Day, or Labor Day. It is only Sunday that can't be a legal holiday. Many people were quite impressed with one Houston merchant who kept egging Christian people on to get more stringent Sunday laws passed. I am sure he was sincere. But we must also reckon with the peculiar legalistic mind that presses the law, as Shylock did, into impossible absurdity.

The newspaper writer also supports my basic thesis by telling us that the first laws regulating Sunday were passed by the first Christian to rule the Roman Empire, Constantine. They have been matters of law ever since that momentous event when Caesar, too, fell under the dominion of Christ. The laws probably became far more strict with the Puritans of Boston. But it is not their rigidity that is under attack now; it is their very existence. Maybe it is true that Christian people have been unconstitutional for over 1600 years; but at least Christian people agreed generally they were right. We were all agreed—Catholic, Protestant, and Eastern Orthodox, to say nothing of the endless splinter groups. The matter is one of simplest reason and an integral part of the Christian structure. It was essential to the national life of Israel and was thoroughly supported by Jesus, although He decried making the Sabbath an end in itself and forcing it to absurdity. The issue really at stake, to be decided by the Supreme Court, is nothing less than whether the Christian system is to be outlawed by the Constitution. Silence hides the fact that it was drawn up to secure a Christian form of government for a Christian people!

The court's decision, when it came, was even more intriguing. It upheld the constitutionality of Sunday closing laws. Then the majority wrote into judicial precedent its opinion which carries immense weight in jurisprudence. The court was careful to explain that no religious considerations were involved: it was simply holding that the states were acting properly in adopting humanitarian laws. It ruled, in effect, that the Sabbath has nothing to do with Creation; the United States government will recognize the law's existence, but is careful to say that it does so only in order to claim for itself official sanction for laws regulating the health and hygiene habits of its subjects.[3]

There is perhaps no purer example of the objectives and methods of those who seek to destroy the created order (status quo) and prepare for a brave new world under man. The stated intent is to repeal God's law which upholds the existing order. Repeal is too drastic, however. Naked power, possesed by the French atheists in the Terror, is not enough. Somehow the Sabbath remains while the earth spins. Besides, such violent action merely arouses desperate resistance. Instead of the gunman, there is a confidence man now at work. He raises the threat and fear of repeal, then smilingly steps back, upholding the law but completely perverting the heart of the matter by falsely interpreting it. Instead of enforcing righteousness to the glory of God, it is now used to pretend to Scriptural sanction for the welfare state.

By eliminating not the law, but the God who gave it, the same law is then twisted to the purpose of the anti-Christ whose government is designed not to punish offenders against God, but to control the lives of men. It is no great leap of thought from gathering the human agencies of government power over individual habits of rest and recreation to totalitarian control in every aspect of life. By seeming to uphold Christian law, the Supreme Court has in fact tried to establish a fraudulent precedent for arrogating to itself and its allied arms of Federal authority, the throne of God himself and cognizance over every detail of every individual's movements. It is hard to see, however, that such ingenious deceit, although it may fool even some of the elect, can alter the truth. It is impossible to enforce the Sabbath without honoring the God who decreed it. The Sabbath is imbedded into the very structure of civilization, and civilization itself must fall with it.

---

[3] Associated Press Reports, May 29, 1961.

FIFTH COMMANDMENT

Honour thy father and thy mother: that thy days may be long upon the land which the Lord thy God giveth thee.

THIS, observes St. Paul, is the first commandment with promise "Honour thy father and mother: . . . that it may be well with thee, and thou mayest live long on the earth."[1] To couch this law in modern speech, we might say it is to the public interest that parents have unrestricted control over their children. The family is the basic unit of society. Therefore, a people made up of strong, well-disciplined families is a strong people that will meet and overcome all the perils that normally face humankind on the earth.

Since we speak of the People of God as the armies of God, we may say that the family is the squad in the Christian army. It is essential to the strength and safety of the army and to the plans and operations of the commander that the files be obedient to the corporal. More than obedience, however, is required by this law. The legal requirement is to "honor." The legal application, as understood in the Bible, is at least twofold: 1) For children, it means absolute dependence and obedience. "The voice of parents is as the voice of God," wrote Shakespeare, "for to children they are heaven's lieutenants." 2) For adults, it means caring for parents in their old age. That Jesus accepted the second phase as well as the first is abundantly clear. He took scribes and Pharisees to task for breach of the commandment by excusing people from care of parents if they made a contribution to the Temple. He Himself, moreover, not only was subject to His parents as a child, but also accepted His responsibility as a man. One of His last acts from the cross was to turn over to His disciple, John, the care of Mary. He saith unto His mother, "Woman, behold thy son." Then saith He to the disciple, "Behold thy mother."

It is virtually impossible to frame laws that spell out in detail how honor and obedience are rendered; therefore, the typical breach of the law is the willful and overt act of cursing father and mother. In taking the scribes and Pharisees to task over this commandment, Jesus recognized the words of the Old Testament as the word of God. He said, "God commanded, saying, He that curseth father or mother, let him die the death."[2] The law of God, confirmed by Christ, exacts the death penalty—from adults, we may presume—for cursing parents. Remember, I am dealing primarily with legal matters. And, we may observe that the only legal obedience required by the law of God is to father and mother. No other authority in this world—certainly not the authority of what we call the state—is supported by unqualified Divine law. The law supporting parental authority is enforced by the death penalty.

There are two or three popular misconceptions that need to be corrected here. One is that the effect of this commandment is somehow to establish a society in which the grand old man of the family holds sway over great swarms of grandchildren and great-grandchildren with their wives and

---

[1] Ephesians 6:2,3.
[2] Matt. 15:4.

husbands and slaves and goods. I have seen respectable writers maintain such a position. It is, however, neither true to the fact nor a correct version. Honor is not commanded to grandparents; obedience is not required of an adult. Rather, when a man takes a wife, he leaves father and mother and cleaves only unto her, according to God's law affirmed by Jesus.[3] Also, since every person has two grandfathers and two grandmothers, to which does he owe obedience? Plainly, no man can serve two masters. Another thing to be noted is the obvious way the commandment refutes the popular misconception that among the ancients women were held as cattle or slaves, or even as real property, to be bought and sold. The calumny, raised by the suffragettes fifty years ago in their rebellion against God's order, is set straight by the Fifth Commandment except, of course, for those perverted minds that will insist the Bible is just a pious cover-up for wicked and deceitful hearts. The high social position of women in Israel is amply testified by the mere existence of this law. Honor thy father and thy mother. No distinction is made. Clearly there could not be in Biblical thought because man and wife are as one flesh. Thus, while obedience is exacted toward two persons, it is two persons who are in fact one flesh. A priest of the Church of England was reported in the press as announcing as is done periodically that the Ten Commandments are out of date and without force today. One of the arguments he advanced was that the ancients viewed wives as property. He said that the Tenth Commandment forbids coveting thy neighbor's wife, and that meant she was owned. However, I believe a man can have a wife as other men don't have her, so that she can be coveted, without the need to regard her in any way as property.

One more thing I am sure I must mention: that is, that no commandment of God may be interpreted as stripping any human being of his due respect as a person. Even parents are not given an authority over their children which would permit them to destroy the children, either physically or morally, or to order them to violate a law of God. Without this law and a careful observance of it, it is hard to see how a people or a nation could last long at all. I know there is an alternative which man can imagine and work toward, and of that more later. For now, let us see for a moment how the spirit of the Fifth Commandment is observed legally today.

To begin with, there are the laws establishing parental relationship, including adoption laws. Many people suppose that children are put out for adoption by that figment of the imagination called the state. But such is not the case. The state has no children, not even unlawful ones. Only fathers and mothers have children. Under the laws of Texas only a mother may give up her child if it is born without a lawful father;

[3] Gen. 2: 24; Matt. 19:5; Mark 10:7.

and if the father has any shadow of claim to being a lawful husband, he must also give his consent. The government may not even designate to whom the child is to go, although many welfare workers would dearly love to pretend they can. A mother has full say; the law upholds her in whatever she may choose to do. It is only when no person with a parental claim may be found that the government may act on its own, and then I daresay possession is more than nine-tenths of the law. Traditionally, it has been the church that receives children for care and nurture, when no other person can be found to accept parental responsibility, in discharge of the command of our Lord to care for widows and orphans. Even the do-gooders admit of this principle in their dole to mothers of illegitimate children—so much per child so that mama can fill her role.

Parental authority is absolute, established in nature, and supported by law based on the commandments of God. I don't know of any laws on our books today exacting a penalty for cursing father or mother. But there are countless laws whose working is meaningless apart from a strict and traditional acceptance of absolute parental authority. While it is true that the law recognizes an age at which a person becomes independent and responsible for himself, the very existence of those laws confirms prior parental control. The fact that a person comes to a legal age says that before that time he was not of age and therefore dependent upon his parents before the law. The legal age may vary slightly from place to place and may vary for different purposes. But the rules are there. Before he comes of age, a person needs consent of his parents to join the army. He needs consent to drive a car or to get a job. He needs consent of his parents to get married or to spend an inheritance. He cannot be held legally responsible for debts incurred without parental consent, and young girls cannot give their consent to any man. On the other hand, parents are held responsible to provide for their children, to train them, and to fit them into the family and so into the social order.

Now I know a great deal about how all people may be inclined to shirk their responsibilities. And I suppose there are some parents who are so unnatural that children cannot survive under their wings. Yet, for thousands of years these people have been so exceptional that no problem whatever exists in dealing with them. That is not to say the world does not have its share of meddlers who have almost a frantic urge to exercise parental responsibilities for others; but it is to say that it is virtually impossible to conceive of any circumstances in which any person who has a child will not give him enough to grow up and make his way on his own. "What man is there of you, whom if his son ask bread, will he give him a stone?"[4]

Neither the church nor the state has any role over any person com-

---

[4] Matt. 7:9.

parable to that of father and mother. Parents are not discharging any government obligation in their parental role, but any government that tries to infringe upon parental authority must be called a "paternalistic," or father-like, government. The one supreme and complete Father is God, the Father of our Lord Jesus Christ by whom all fatherhood is known. His image is the framework for individual men and women to grow up into as they beget offspring—not into any lifeless institution or any temporal government. Governments, under God, exist not to supplant fatherhood but to protect it, exist upon it, and punish those who abuse its privileges and responsibilities. So may thy days as a people be long upon the land which the Lord thy God giveth thee. The Church of God exists, not to replace fathers and mothers (although we speak of our fathers in God and have god-fathers and god-mothers), but to support them. Church and state are each and both geared to parenthood by the law of the same God who established both church and state. They must operate within and by consent of fatherhood and motherhood. Such is the law given through the church to be enforced by the state.

So much for the meaning of the Fifth Commandment and its expression in the laws of Texas and other states today as part of all Christendom. It remains to show how this law is under attack by the so-called liberal movement and what alternative is offered by the attackers. I think it is most profitable to begin by considering that the need for children to be reared under adult supervision is so required in nature that no effort to demolish parental authority could even be entertained without at the same time offering at least an imagined substitute. The full implication of various propaganda efforts today to weaken or destroy respect for parents is lost unless we are aware that the supposed substitute for father and mother is ready and waiting and presupposed by all family wreckers. That alternative is as old as human writing on the subject. Plato spelled it out in his treatise, *The Republic*. That was before our Redemption. Plato here is the social planner of all social planners and is describing the plans and specifications for the ideal state. To him the state is itself one great family, and all being and activity are bent toward the interests of the state. In order to follow practices of good breeding, the best stock will be used, says he, for that purpose, both male and female. The less worthy can mate by drawing lots from time to time. When children are born, says Plato, ". . . the proper officers will take the offspring of the good parents to the pen or fold, and there they will deposit them with certain nurses . . . The offspring of the inferior will be put away in some mysterious or unknown place."

"But how will they know who are fathers and daughters?" asks Plato's straight man.

"They will never know," is the sage's answer. "Such is the scheme,

Glaucon, according to which the guardians of our State are to have their wives and families in common."[5]

So Plato details the lie in order to pretend that the state has children. By pulling families apart the state usurps parental authority, children are bred like cattle for state purposes, women are treated exactly like men, numbers are controlled to prevent population explosion, and society is regulated by human laws and actions. Now even Plato had the grace to see that his fantastic monster had within itself the seeds of its own destruction. Yet, he concluded it was worth the try, and so have other men ever since. The pattern has never been altered. The concept is full blown the moment one introduces the notion that the state encompasses the body politic, that all life must serve the ends of the state, and that the state, not fathers and mothers, has children.

It is no accident and nothing new that the communes clamped on the suffering human beings of China are nothing more nor less than Plato's famous pens for women and children—the common chattel of the state. Today in China, family life, the bulwark of Chinese society as of any other, is systematically being ground to pieces in the interests of a mammoth monster state in which husbands and wives and children exist, but all recognizable family privilege and responsibility are swallowed up in communism. Plainly neither Marx nor the Russian Soviet nor yet the Chinese Reds dreamed up the system. Old Plato squeezed the concept out to the last drop, and it has been advocated in varying degrees of completeness by every socialist or liberal movement the world has ever known. Adolph Hitler seized wives for the state, penned up brood males for the state, and herded children into youth groups that looked to the state, not parents, for authority. Old Ben Lindsey in Denver years ago dreamed up what he called juvenile courts to take away parental supervision; and he advocated something called companionate marriage: legal wife-shopping. Divorce laws have been systematically weakened to the point of scrambled eggs in every state.

The National Council of Churches has conducted in many cities a television program called Talk Back, the format of which is to put family ties up to judgment before the general public by the demoralizing blathering of high school students. Youth movements everywhere have no object of existence except to replace parental control. Every police state must institute a youth spy system in which boys and girls report to a government official on the loyalty of their parents. Children are made to feel different and inadequate, positively guilty, if they fail to assert their independence and to be different from the old fogies. All of this to the end of trying to wrench from God His ordering of life and His control over mankind, and

---

[5] Plato, *The Republic*, Book 5.

to vest it in what one liberal clergyman said for the National Council of Churches is the only public institution under God—the state.

The effect of weakening parental supervision—increasing crime and violence—is almost automatic. I never heard a person charged with punishing crime who did not agree that all so-called juvenile crime is a product of weak parental supervision. There never has been any substitute for parents, not even the mythical beast, the state. All this sounds most frightening and horrible—a reality we must admit in far and distant lands, but nothing we in the United States are facing, we think. And yet the rate of juvenile violence, insanity, and suicide in this country is alarming. And if we look close, we discover that the whole monster is inherent in the school system which has been gradually, if relentlessly, clamped upon us. The system of so-called public schools—a name, incidentally, of recent application—begins and ends with the proposition that children are born to serve the ends of the state.

Some years ago Winston Churchill's son was quoted as saying in Colorado Springs that Americans had no cause to find fault with British socialism. He admitted that Britain had gone a long way down the road, but he said with some acid that even Britain had nothing as socialistic, or communistic, as the American government school system. It is built on the proposition that parents cannot be entrusted with the schooling of their children and therefore are compelled by law to send them to schools they are compelled by law to pay for, but which the government controls.

Some of you may think I am toying with words to call the so-called public schools government schools. Let me give you the definition of public schools officially published by the United States Department of Health, Education, and Welfare in one of its pamphlets: "A 'public' school is the creature of the state and is subject not only to the state's regulatory controls but is under immediate operational control of a governmental agency or agent. A 'public' school is supported and maintained at public expense (meaning taxation exacted by force)."[6] In another publication of this same agency it is said, "The goal of having every physically and mentally able child of elementary and secondary school age enrolled in United States' schools has not yet been realized."[7] Only ninety-seven out of one hundred had been caught by 1958. Can't you see the truant officers, the police, the army, and the navy ferreting out the swimming holes of the South, the back alleys of New York City, the hills of Tennessee, and the estates of men of immense wealth, to find those three unaccounted-for urchins?

Government instead of fathers and mothers is not a new idea. It was

---

[6] *The State and Non-Public Schools,* U. S. Department of Health, Education and Welfare, Office of Education, 1958; p. 1.
[7] *State Legislation on School Attendance,* U. S. Department of Health, Education and Welfare, Office of Education, 1960, p. 23.

inherent in what Horace Mann did as part of the Unitarian rebellion in New England. As early as 1820, advocates of government schools and compulsory attendance argued from the premise that the state had prior rights in the matter and for its own ends had to see to it that all children were schooled under its supervision. As early as 1831 the traditional or orthodox Christians were publicly voicing their apprehensions that some people were making "their zeal for education a cover for their attack on the Christian religion." Then the fight was to keep instruction in basic Christian religion and morals and Bible reading in the school. Today even Bible reading would be outlawed under a suit brought in Florida.

In California in 1886 one Zach. Montgomery, a man who later was made assistant attorney general of the United States, published a vigorous assault on the government school system as destroying parental control.[8] He marshalled overwhelming statistics to show that the expected increase in juvenile crime was in fact following at an alarming rate upon the introduction of the compulsory school program from coast to coast. He also cited the Biennial Report of Mr. John Swett, California State Superintendent of Public Instruction in 1864, that parents must step aside for state teachers. "The vulgar impression that parents have a legal right to dictate to teachers is entirely erroneous . . . If the teacher's conduct is approved by his employers, the parents have no remedy against him or them." The California penal code in 1886, according to Mr. Montgomery, made it a criminal offense for any parent to even insult a teacher of a public school in the presence or hearing of a pupil thereof. So from a people who put to death one who curses father or mother, we move to one that punishes father or mother who insults a public school teacher.

Today, when the monster of a government school system is all but three per cent complete and central control is soon to be moved to Washington, parents may look around them and see the price. Children by universal admission are unlearned. They are, for example, seeking permission to do graduate study in universities without being able to express themselves in writing or without the mental equipment to read a popular political pamphlet, *The Federalist Papers,* written for teamsters and farmers in 1776. Moreover, whereas the advocates of universal compulsory schooling claimed the resulting decrease in crime would pay the cost of schools, crime is still zooming up. The crime, suicide, and insanity rate in this country today has reached proportions never dreamed of 150 years ago and far exceeding that of such nations as Mexico. By every conceivable test the government school system is a criminal failure: it has not taught; it has demolished morals; the Christian religion is virtually unknown even by many clergymen, and our nation is unable even to see to its own interests at home and abroad.

---

[8] Montgomery, Zach., *The School Question,* Gibson Bros., Washington, D. C., 1886.

Only in one area is the system nearing its admitted goal. Nearly every urchin in the land has been seized by its claws and is held squirming and squealing in an iron grip. The state has its children, and it doesn't even have to see to their food and shelter, as Plato asked. Father and mother meekly see to that, but are powerless to see to what their own children learn. A person like myself, who believes parents should have full responsibility for the schooling or training of any kind of their own children and who offers a church school to open a little area of choice to some parents, is branded by a California professor as subversive. And our own church raises the question in a conference of whether it might be a curse for the church to be in education—whatever it means to be "in education." The political and anti-Christian slant of all public school textbooks is notorious, and you and I know from bitter personal experience the ordinary fund of knowledge and mental discipline we were never exposed to.

In some ways Plato and the Chinese Communists are pikers. We have instituted a system of enslaving our own children to the all-powerful myth called the state; and we will fight to keep it that way instead of to recover an ounce of parental authority as commanded by the law of God. In 1886 every standard writer on the subject of either law or morals agreed that parents are bound by all that is holy to see to the education of their children. Bovier, Chancellor Kent and Sir William Blackstone might be quoted. Today I don't know who does much writing on any of these subjects. But those who do are proceeding apace on the proposition that the Fifth Commandment, along with the rest of the great moral structure of Godly law, will be forgotten, and the state must see to it. Government officials are to have sole responsibility for the training of the young, and parents may be penned up in their respective communes if the Washington authorities deem it to be in the interest of the state.

Yet our law still resounds with the thunder of Heaven: "Honour thy father and thy mother, that thy days may be long upon the land which the Lord thy God giveth thee."

SIXTH COMMANDMENT

Thou shalt do no murder.

A T THIS point we come to the crux of the law. The first five of the Ten Commandments—the first half—have to do with legal support for public honor to God and to God's agents, parents. The last five have to do with legal support for respect to all men. By the Sixth Commandment, man's station in the hierarchy of Creation is secured, just as God's is legally recognized by the First Commandment. All rightness toward God is grounded upon strict, uncompromising observance of the First Commandment, "Thou shalt have no other gods before me." It is thereby against the law to put anybody or anything before God.

In the same way, all rightness toward other human beings is grounded upon strict, uncompromising observance of the Sixth Commandment, "Thou shalt do no murder." Like the preceding laws, it is implicit in Creation long before Moses. It was explicit beginning with Noah. It is against the law for any creature to arrogate to himself power or authority over the life of a human being. To be endowed with human nature, that is, to be born of a woman, is to possess a rank higher than all other creatures except angels and to inherit a hope even of exceeding them in glory. No finer expression of man's place in the universe can be found than in the Eighth Psalm:

"What is man, that thou art mindful of him?
    and the son of man, that thou visitest him?
For thou hast made him a little lower than the angels,
    and hast crowned him with glory and honour.

Thou madest him to have dominion over the works of thy hands;
    thou hast put all things under his feet:

All sheep and oxen; yea, and the beasts of the field;
    the fowl of the air, and the fish of the sea and
    whatsoever passeth through the path of the seas.

O Lord our Lord, how excellent is thy name in all the earth."

So far we have little difficulty. Even though some shifty scientist appears from time to time to tell us that man's dominion over all creation is mere happenstance, and that it could any day fall to the insects to supersede man, nobody would deny, I am sure, that human nature now rules not only the earth but perhaps also the skies. Some take the matter out of the hands of that blind and stupid goddess of chance and would say that man has conquered nature. And while that makes more sense than the idea of sheer luck, it also recognizes the central point that man is on top. We Christians take a far more sober view: God made us that way, and He gave us dominion. God's final act in the original six days of Creation was to make man, its crowning glory. "And God said, Let us make man in our image, after our likeness: and let them have dominion over the fish of the sea, and over the fowl of the air, and over the cattle, and over all the earth, and

73

over every creeping thing that creepeth upon the earth."[1] Adam exercised his rule by giving a name to everything. "Whatsoever Adam called every living creature, that was the name thereof."[2] After the Flood, when God wiped out the evil generation of the earth and gave man a new start through Noah, God renewed his command putting man in charge. "The fear of you and the dread of you shall be upon every beast of the earth, and upon every fowl of the air, upon all that moveth upon the earth, and upon all the fishes of the sea; into your hand are they delivered."[3] So it is by God's settled command that man rules all the earth. But however we account for it, the fact that it must be accounted for testifies to the truth of the fact: it is really beyond doubt.

Next we must consider what we mean when we speak of this man who has dominion over all the earth. Much hangs upon how we clarify that point. Today there is an almost universally widespread piece of fuzzy thinking that assumes the most mature and intelligent understanding to be that by "man" we mean the composite of the whole human race. Mankind, or human kind, is the jargon. Precise thinking required of Christians cannot tolerate any such notion. We can somehow grasp an ethereal abstraction which we might call humanity: it is probably what Plato was describing as pure *idea*. Probably a still better understanding can be found in the doctrine of angels. The pure, unsullied, complete expression of man-ness—the ideal pattern of the Son of Man—is something that belongs to the angelic order of Creation, not to this world. Actually, when we speak of man, we mean *a* man. Human nature is complete in every single human being that ever lived, even those unfortunates who have some congenital handicap. It is not good for man to live alone. But human nature is fully and completely expressed in every individual. Adam was complete. Adam is man. Adam is the whole human race. He is the father of all living. From him we inherit not only the pattern of humanity restored by Christ, but we inherit its fallen and sinful nature which Adam passed on.

Our brotherhood with all other human beings is the brotherhood from our Father Adam which is a brotherhood in a common condemnation: we have all sinned and come short of the glory God intended for us. Right here we meet one of the first steps of heresy and faulty reasoning. Someone will say that God made male and female, so that it takes two at least to express human nature. Now we must be careful. Pure humanity, pure human nature, is not identical with the human race. It is true that mankind now is male and female. But the Bible is careful to secure the basic truth that human nature in a woman is the same as it is in a man, and it is complete in each. Adam was alone. He was all mankind. And the Bible carefully records that God saw it was not good for Adam to be alone: he

[1] Gen. 1:26.
[2] Gen. 2:19.
[3] Gen. 9:2.

could find no helpmate among the creatures he named; so God took a rib from Adam and out of his person made Eve, his wife. Thus neither Adam nor Eve could live a good life alone; they needed each other in this world. But each is fully human. There has been much respectable guessing on the point that Adam actually was created with the full power to reproduce his kind: somehow he was what we would call bi-sexual. Whether that be quite what the Bible says or not I would not argue. But it is abundantly clear that Adam possessed within his single person the fullness of the whole of mankind. I think it is rather curious that those tender souls who recoil at the genetic difficulties involved in the sons of Adam marrying their sisters really must stick harder at the realization that Eve herself came out of Adam. There is no biological difficulty at all in the matter. The ban against incest is not chiefly for biological reasons, but for spiritual reasons. It applies to adopted children, stepchildren, and in-laws quite as fiercely as to blood kin. It is clear, then, that in the beginning human nature was complete in a single individual person.

It is equally clear that such will be the case when human nature is fully realized by those who at last achieve to the fullness of the stature of Christ. Human destiny is to come to Heaven individually having been made perfect in Jesus Christ, the second Adam who arrived at His destiny of resurrection and ascension to Heaven. For in the resurrection, said Jesus, they neither marry, nor are given in marriage, but are as the angels of God in Heaven (that is, complete and sexless). Manhood, or humanness, is complete in every individual person, male or female. True enough, in this world we humans must, as part of our training for Heaven, learn to live with each other. We must learn the principle of subordination, and we do so under earthly conditions which begin with marriage and extend with endless ramification. But the essence of this creature man, this amazing being who was made a little lower than the angels and yet is to be crowned with glory and worship, is complete in each one of us.

I cannot help being a little amused at our groupy friends—you know, those with the intellectual limp that requires them to speak of humanity in the mass, as an abstraction of the race in its entirety. For all they do is to try to subsume every living person into a mammoth personality. The nation is given a personality; the race is personalized. We have Uncle Sam, a single person. We have John Bull for England and Marianne for France. There is the greater Scriptural precedent of speaking of the Hebrew people as Jacob, or Israel. They speak of the whole race as a single personality, having a childhood and an old age: Adam, again. As a matter of fact, it is almost certainly true that the human mind cannot reach to comprehension of anything higher than that of a single human personality. There is no more difficult leap of thought than the doctrine of the Trinity by which we understand the nature of God to be more than a person.

75

Thus God, whom we cannot see for ourselves, we can know is three persons in one Being—Father, Son, and Holy Ghost. We can know that it is so by being told. But it is most unlikely that we can do any more than repeat the information. We still know the Father only by knowing one person—the Son, Jesus Christ. Thus, every human life shares equally in the dominion which man has over the earth. In that, all men are equal: we are not equally ranked under God, but equally ranked over nature.

The dominion of mankind is maintained by preserving the dominion of every single person. The principle is easy to grasp for every man of experience. When Britain ruled the world, for example, the whole might of the empire was called upon to maintain the power of every single Englishman. Even we of the United States have known what it means to protect the power and prestige of the nation by being ready to go to war to defend or avenge a single citizen. It is no accident that Castro both defies the United States government and manhandles our citizens. One act is of a piece with the other. So the nations grant extra-territorial rights to nationals of foreign governments with equal power and prestige: these foreign governments have no dominion over either the other government or its citizens.

So much for man being realized full in every individual. There remains to consider the principle of dominion. We all know, I am sure, what dominion means generally. But there are many things it entails. One of them is the power to give a name. Every child knows that it can name its own doll or its own dog. A boy who can't name his dog doesn't own a dog. Adam gave names to all things, and thus he gave us speech and language. You know, it is impossible to establish a language by any other than one person. If Eve had given her names to the creatures and Adam his, there would have been two languages, and Adam and Eve couldn't have fussed with each other any better than before. But no matter: giving names is one act of dominion and rule and ownership. Another is to bear responsibility for and to train and teach those under you. One is accountable to God for all that has been given under his dominion or into his hand.

Another expression of dominion in this world is the power of death. I can't for the life of me imagine why people today try so desperately to obscure the reality of the power inherent in the mere strength to kill. To take away the life of any creature is to exercise the last word in dominion or rule over the creature, except God's word, which is to give life in the first place, and can raise us from the dead. God has required us to exist by giving us existence: no man had any choice in the matter, either as to when and where he would be born, or who would be his parents, or what worldly heritage would be his. But the very next ranking power is given into the hands of every man: the power of death. The combination of physical, mental, and willful powers in every single human being add up to the physical power in each one of us to take the life of any other living creature. True, there is a risk involved. And some creatures can and do kill men. Some even are reputed to attack human beings without provocation: man killers, like sharks, tigers, hyenas, and copperheads. But if the dominion of man is to be maintained on the earth, then individual men must avenge the death of any other man. Not only must the particular shark that killed a man be killed, or the particular lion or tiger, but sharks and lions and tigers as such simply because they rebel against the fear of man and the dread of man that has been put upon them.

Man, to maintain his dominion, must from time to time prove himself. It seems to me this principle is so basic that no person is qualified to discuss matters of government, order, discipline, subordination, or even human relations, who doesn't almost instinctively know it. The last enemy, said St. Paul, is death. Death puts an end to the pretentions of every creature. "Then cometh the end when he (Christ) shall have delivered up the kingdom to God, even the Father; when he shall have put down all rule and all authority and power. For he must reign, till he hath put all enemies under his feet. The last enemy that shall be destroyed is death."[4]

Since death and the power of death came into the world under Adam, Adam in his exercise of dominion must also hold in his hands the last act of death. God said to Noah, "And surely your blood of your lives will I require; at the hand of every beast will I require it, and at the hand of man; at the hand of every man's brother will I require the life of man. Whoso sheddeth man's blood, by man shall his blood be shed: for in the image of God made he man."[5] It is insufferable that the life of any man shall be taken by any other creature, including another man. But if it is done, then man, who is the supreme authority in the world and who must maintain his own dominion, must be the one to take vengeance. Broken laws must be repaired.

The power of death is the supreme power of temporal rule: it belongs to God and is delegated to man. The Lord killeth, and the Lord maketh alive. If that offends your sensibilities, I am sorry. That is the way of it. And that is what it means that human life has a high price in our civilization. The price is another human life. When a human life can be paid for by a fine, as it can among non-Christian peoples, or when it can be paid for by a few years of enforced confinement, as it is among us all too often, life is cheap. Maybe some people like it that way. I recall one who did, the late Agnes Smedley, a dedicated socialist, who was so appalled by conditions in heathen China that she was physically sick. But she still wanted a social order in which there is no blood vengeance for a man. All over the world our "do-gooders" are shocked by conditions among

---

[4] I Cor. 15:24-26.
[5] Gen. 9:5,6.

those people who are not Christian and who have no capital punishment: where babies are exposed to die, accidental deaths are as common as those to dogs and chickens on a modern highway, and throats are slit daily for a quarter. Sometimes people even today seek a cash settlement for a man's life. I understand there is almost a formula by which a man's earning power may be calculated and his widow and heirs compensated by what he might have earned if he had lived. Suppose it is a million dollars. The value is cheap. It is as cheap as the thirty shekels at which they valued the life of Jesus.

The commandment against murder was and is interpreted to include manslaughter and accidental killings, although the harshness was mitigated from the beginning by providing sanctuaries and escapes for those guilty of unpremeditated killings. The dominion of man is secure only as long as man exercises the power of death to avenge crimes against his own dominion and security under the law of God. Now today those who writhe and twist under God's established order, who would rebel at the way God set up creation and reorder it their own way, cannot stomach the awfulness of their own responsibility to exact vengeance. For just as the man to be avenged is humanity fully, so no individual can really delegate the responsibility for vengeance. Ultimately it comes down to the act of an individual—the hangman, the headsman, or the man who pulls the switch on the electric chair. "At the hand of every man's brother" God requires the blood of man.

In recognition of the awfulness of this responsibility, executions among Christians are normally in public. Our liberal do-gooders froth and fume and rage about how people who go to public executions are blood-thirsty, morbid thrill hunters, besporting themselves like the Romans at the circus. Maybe so. But I don't think any person who makes such an ass of himself with that kind of braying ever attended a public hanging. If he had, he would realize he was lying in his teeth or else was himself such a monster that he himself took such a lighthearted pleasure in the spectacle. No, there is no fun in an execution, ever. But by it every person shares in his own responsibility, both for the crime and for the vengeance. It is as solemn and horrible a duty as jury duty, a heavier obligation than voting (or *not* voting). Executions in Israel were by stoning, so that every responsible person actually took a hand in the vengeance. I can think of no experience more sobering to any human. To attribute to other people savage thirst for blood is to demean even fallen man and debase the Creator and His creature to the point of blasphemy. People just don't kill other people lightly. Certainly not those people who are law abiding, responsible, disciplined and orderly people. Why we should suddenly suppose the murderer has become precious and that the poor chief of police and the public prosecutor and the happy-go-lucky public are the ones with bloody hands I will never know. It may be, of course, that those with murder in their hearts have a passionate sympathy and respect for real killers, those who have had the courage to go all the way with their rebellion against God. But I am not one to enjoy a hanging. I have known hard-boiled newspapermen to vomit after witnessing an execution. And I don't believe my God-fearing, respectable fellows and neighbors are any different. I think it is a good thing when we have to watch such a grim business and have it impressed upon us that each of us as an individual man was made in the image of God Himself, is responsible for dominion over all the earth, and must be prepared to uphold human dominion even, if need be, with his own hand. That is the way God has defined crime and the way He has ordered its punishment.

Now there is an alternative to God's way being offered. There are those who are attacking this law right now in Texas and all the rest of Christendom in order to complete their great rebellion against the dominion of Jesus Christ. These people would make human life cheap again, take dominion away from the individual man under God, and place it in some mysterious imaginary power called the state. They would place final sovereignty and dominion, not in God the Creater, but in this beast called the state which men manipulate and which always must be the equipage of a single man. That man, the leader, would be instructed by these people to defy God's commandment and to abolish capital punishment. This state ruler would thus take it upon himself to redefine crime and to recodify the laws. It is not, he would say, the final act of rebellion to kill a man: only to resist the state. Says he, you may kill another man and pay it out by fine or long imprisonment or maybe just a slap on the wrist. Why? Because no individual inherits the dominion of the earth except the World Ruler and His ministers. Him you may not even question, let alone kill. You may not resist the jailer, the policeman, the judge, the legislator, or any official. But the private citizen—well, just be careful and promise you won't do it too often.

Weak sisters everywhere are bleeding profusely from the heart for the poor murderers, and on those wicked officials who assume the God-given duty of avenging the death of a man, they pour out scorn and abuse. But remember the whole structure of criminal law is demolished when murder is no longer a capital offense. At that moment the state has arrogated to itself the right and the power to define what is crime, and it becomes unjust by refusing just penalties. If the state can define crime as well as punish it, then all crime is by definition political. There is then no crime except crime against the state. Justice is dead. It is not mere coincidence that in Israel and Soviet Russia there is no capital punishment except for the murder of a jailer. But Israel can put anybody to death for belittling a Jew anywhere in the world. I don't know on what grounds the Russians murder their citizens. Nor do I know what means this bleeding heart state is going to use to eliminate those undesirable citizens it is always talking about eliminating, unless it will kill them. But then, you see, that is not capital punishment. It is not even punishment. There is no crime—only the duty of regulating all lives.

The big drive is on all over the world to abolish capital punishment. When it is done, the whole concept of crime is gone, and the world-state is a necessity; socialism is an accomplished fact awaiting only the intervention of Christ Himself and the end of the world; and you and I are in for horrors beyond imagination. The sovereign protection of the State of Texas, which now rather shakily stands between us and the will of a Supreme Court which has already decided it is criminal to oppose its decree, will be gone. Raw individual force will be the last resort, and you and I as individual humans will be called upon for heroics we have never dreamed of. I hope and pray each one of us will fill the bill; but let us first do all in our power to forestall the debacle as long as we can. Let us not wait until the storm trooper appears in the bedroom to lock the door or even stand guard outside with brave Christian men. We must turn back this monstrous defiance of God, of law, of justice, of order, decency, and reverence for human life. The Devil is aroused, his breath is hot, and his henchmen are legion. They are pulpit weepers, and executive secretaries of high-sounding front organizations, and magazine writers and editors: all of them remonstrate nobly about their offended sensibilities in the hangman, but none has a word to say about what he is really doing— replacing God's law with an arbitrary human being who calls himself god and himself regulates all life—without justice. God has decreed that whoso sheddeth man's blood, by man shall his blood be shed.

SEVENTH COMMANDMENT

Thou shalt not commit adultery.

I DON'T think I exaggerate when I say that to many people this commandment is the one they think of as the whole Ten Commandments. Some years ago when I distributed some mimeographed copies of the book that was later published as *Sacred Studies* and I announced that it dealt with the Ten Commandments, I noticed people outside the church eagerly thumbing through their folders. I was so pleased at the evident interest I had to peek to see what they were reading. They had turned right away to the Seventh Commandment. There may have been a little letdown for some as the treatment did not emphasize the matters of chastity and lust, but rather dealt quite properly, as I intend to do now, with the legal support for the holy bond of matrimony.

This commandment has to do with violation of the marriage bond. And that's all. That's enough, I am sure. But I think it is a mistake to stretch it to cover the whole vast and important field of purity. Christians certainly insist upon chastity in and out of marriage: for God did not call us to uncleanness, but to holiness. There isn't much the law can do about purity and holiness. But the law can and does punish adulterers.

A near-tragic incident growing out of stretching this law too far was told me by a strong Christian mother. It had to do with her son, a young man who, as so often happens, was exposed in high school to a very evil teacher who went out of his way to sweet talk young men and women into scorn and mockery of the Christian faith and to tear them into confused and distracted men and women committed to the worship of government. The approach with this young man was simply to point out that the Seventh Commandment does apply only to violation of marriage—not to the conduct of other people. Since that much was true and at the same time different from what the young man had been taught, he was then a patsy for going all the way to the proposition that everything he had been taught in Sunday School was unreliable. Of course there was more to the treatment, but the boy was broken at this point. It was years before he got back on his feet again. Fortunately, this young man did. All too many don't. Now I don't for a moment think every child who is taught incorrectly about the Seventh Commandment will have that experience. But the story does show the importance of being precise with these things and sticking to the point. Law is law and as such has an exalted role in life. But it is only law and can't be made a code of morals or a ladder to Heaven.

We have already seen, in dealing with the Fifth Commandment, that God's law marks out the natural family as the unit of society. "The voice of parents is as the voice of God, for to children they are heaven's lieutenants." A people among whom children obey their parents and adults honor them and provide for them in old age is a strong resilient people that can rise to overcome the storms of life and will live long in the land.

But it is not only the honoring of parents that is required to have strong families. Husbands and wives must be exclusively loyal to each other. Marriage is certainly an essential condition for a family: to invade a marriage and break the bond between husband and wife is to threaten the whole structure of society and human life. Adultery always brings immediate threat of murder and violence, it casts a fearful cloud on a whole community, and it is one of the most serious of crimes. Like all the other Ten Commandments, it drew the death penalty in Biblical times.

Adultery is so serious that we will do well to consider again here the institution of marriage itself. It is true that in marriage a man and a woman are, as our Lord said, one flesh. That in and of itself, however, does not constitute a marriage. The union of the flesh can happen under other circumstances (for which we have other names), and it does not make a marriage. St. Paul asks, "Know ye not that he which is joined to an harlot is one body?"[1] Adultery itself is a case in point. Rape is another. Marriage is something else. The essence of marriage is the exchange of vows and the mutual bond that is thereby established. The bond is made publicly. The vows are of the most solemn and sacred kind. They are made explicitly before God and in the face of the general public. In the words of the Episcopal service we say, "Forasmuch as M—and N—have consented together in holy wedlock, and have witnessed the same before God and this company, and thereto have given and pledged their troth, each to the other . . . I pronounce that they are Man and Wife . . ." *Public witness to mutual consent and pledges of troth:* these are the things that make a marriage.

The integrity of the whole moral argument of the Ten Commandments begins to stand out even more clearly in this. The mystery of making and keeping a pledge of loyalty, a promise, to God, to a spouse; the taking of the name of God in a solemn oath: these are the things upon which the moral law is built. These are the foundations of society. These are the things that are kept alive and in force by the inflicting of penalties for breaking them. Promises, vows, pledges, loyalties all vanish if they are broken with impunity. Society turns on keeping pledges and punishing violations. Credit is an extension of the principle into the business world. The contract is established by a spoken word, and is no better than that word. The bond of loyalty or the effect of a pledge lies in what we might call the spirit world: it has no shape or weight or size; it cannot be touched, seen, or heard. But it controls human life.

What an adulterer really does is to break a particular solemn vow. By his act he tramples upon marriage itself, mocks God and society, and figuratively tosses that particular promise into the trash can, making it of no value. I am sure I do not need to tell you there are many criminal

---

[1] I Cor. 6:16.

laws in every state designed to bring wrath down upon the head of every adulterer. The breaking of marriage by adultery is possible even in polygamous societies—witness the notorious case of David and Bath-Sheba. But with us Christian people the marriage vow is a return to the exclusive monogamy of Adam and Eve—as it was from the beginning. Each partner vows not only loyalty but exclusive loyalty—keeping only unto her, and only unto him, as long as ye both shall live. I really think many people today would do much better to call a policeman than a divorce lawyer in cases of a false spouse. We have learned bitterly that divorce only complicates matters: the Old Testament death penalty accomplished the end of setting the innocent party free and removed the complications of multiple marriages. That may be too drastic for us, but all the same the police today are equipped to deal with the matter.

I must turn aside for a moment to consider the oh-so-much-abused story in John's Gospel about how some men brought to Jesus a woman taken in adultery and He said, "He that is without sin among you, let him first cast a stone at her."[2] I have heard that story used in the Council of the Diocese of Texas to defend the sponsorship of a Communist speaker in a church meeting. Now the story is perfectly clear and consistent with Jesus' rigid demands upon all men. Jesus simply refused to assume the role of king, judge, or policeman. He refused again and again. Again and again, after Satan himself failed, the crowds, the people, tried to seize Him and make Him a king to rule with the power of this world. A young man tried to make Him decide an inheritance case. Jesus replied, "Man, who made me a judge or a divider over you?"[3] The men who caught a woman in the act of adultery were trying to trump up an accusation of rebellion against Jesus. They brought her to Him to judge and condemn and sentence to stoning. It was a trap: a dangerous one, because He was suspected of laying the groundwork for an uprising. For Him to refuse to give judgment would seem to violate God's own law; to give it would displace Caesar. But Jesus turned the trick back on His tempters as He was to do so many other times. "Hath no man condemned thee? Neither do I condemn thee." The Son of Man came not to destroy, but to save. "Go and sin no more." The woman was exposed, caught, convicted—but the rule of Christ was not that of the world to punish, but to use His own power to forgive. It is the Son of Man who has power on earth to forgive sins—not the judge or the policeman. But the Son of Man cannot forgive if He acts as judge and policeman.

To this day it is no different. No person coming to a priest to confess this or another sin will be punished or even turned over to state authorities by the priest. The priest's hands are made for blessing, not for beating. One does not appeal to a Christian minister for justice, judgment, or con-

[2] John 8:3 ff.
[3] Luke 12:14.

85

demnation, but for forgiveness. But neither does one appeal to a judge for forgiveness. The two functions are by their nature forever separate and are united only in the Risen Christ and the Holy Trinity. The judge, who serves under Christ in this world for wrath, is still required to punish any criminal brought before him. The law is still with us.[4]

I must now turn to the matter of how God's law forbidding adultery is today under attack. The attack began long ago. I say long ago, yet it has been within my own lifetime that it has been so vigorous. As recently as World War I, social pressure in the United States was still strong enough that marriage was unquestioned as a life-long union of man and wife under God. Conversely, divorce was a scandal. True, divorce was not unknown, but it was mostly confined to Hollywood and New York high society and was always shocking. Statistics, which I have not bothered to assemble because they are all too familiar, give eloquent testimony of the changing spirit. But the change was not spontaneous or accidental. It came as the result of vicious and angry propaganda all wrapped up with something called the woman movement and aimed at breaking down the supposed hypocrisy of good people.

The free love cults, which in the nineteenth century were confined to a few intellectual cranks, filtered down in the general disillusionment of "Over There" in World War I to popular acceptance. Hollywood took an old theme of romantic literature, the theme of unrequited adulterous passion culminating in death, and reworked it with a happy ending. The love of love, the love of desire for its own sake, which is the mark of the longing for someone married to another, was the subject of romantic troubadour ballads in the High Middle Ages. These troubadours were probably priests of the vicious Albigensian heresy, the architects of courtly love and its deadly consequences. But at least their theme was true: those who cultivated desire for its own sake, a desire that must be crushed by satisfaction, carried the theme to its appointed end—death. The arch-type of the romantic ballad, *Tristan and Isolde,* begins with the lines, "I sing you a song of love and death." The song continues through endless adventures that are remarkably like those of the familiar radio soap opera, always flitting around the desire of people for someone whose love they cannot

---

[4] It is interesting to take note of the confusion of church and state as shown in the word "penitentiary," which is an institution where criminals may be confined for a period of time instead of being punished. The word originally was attached to institutions of the church. The reason is obvious. It is in the church where men do penance and where penitents are recognizd and have a status of their own. Often today in Roman Catholic countries the penitents still, as they did in the early church, wear special clothing and sit in a special place in church. Criminals used to be turned over by the state to the church where they would be given the opportunity to make public confession, offer restitution and go through a period of discipline designed to strengthen their moral character to the point where they could return to full participation in the life of free men. While in the care of the church they were housed in penitentiaries. In our country, however, men are forced by the threat of government power to enter into penitentiaries. That arm of our society which is supposed to function as the wrath of God also attempts to correct men. So we are confronted with the amazing spectacle of penitents who are such, not out of a heart of true repentance, but because they are forced to be at gun point. Thus nobody is either punished or forgiven. Men are just hardened, embittered, branded, and schooled in advanced criminal arts. Yet the Christian option dies hard, and somehow even we who have forgotten the origin of penitentiaries still expect that men confined in them will somehow mend their lives.

requite because they are married to someone else. But eventually even this theme wears out, the lovers do breach the walls, and then the desire, on which they have fed so long, has been fulfilled and their ruling passion demolished. The end, then, is tragic death. A more popular illustration is the wailing ballad of lost lovers in early American song—the jailbird, the girl drowned in the bloom of youth, and so on.

Hollywood has made a significant and violent wrench in the theme. This illicit and dark desire for forbidden fruit was transformed into the seed bed for living happily ever after. All that was required was for the pale and sickly lovers to get a divorce and remarry—and, like old fairy tale characters, to achieve full married bliss, a bliss unknown and supposedly unknowable to those dutiful souls who kept their marriage bonds in the drudgery of daily routine and ordinary loyalty and fulfillment. People took that new theme seriously in the '20s. From coast to coast states loosened up their divorce laws. Judge Ben Lindsey, who thought that justice ought to be withheld from teenage criminals and that they should have special courts called juvenile (I think the judges were supposed to be juvenile, really), also thought young people should have the opportunity for what he called companionate marriage. That is, they would enter into marriage with admitted reservations—just to try it for a while. He so shocked the sensibilities of the city of Denver that he soon had to leave, but behind him he left his evil seed which soon grew into the same thing without legal sanctions. It simply became quite acceptable to take the solemn marriage vows with mental reservations.

I think another phase of the propaganda was far more devastating even than the Hollywood divorce-for-happiness theme. It was the work of those who followed John Dewey's philosophy, built upon Darwin's mad hypothesis of evolution, which held that human beings are nothing but products of nature, and that in our nature there are urges and appetites, of which sex is foremost, which must be satisfied. That notion invaded schoolroom, church, doctor's office, institution and college. Man is a beast, we were told, and, if his beastly nature is not appeased, his character will be twisted and distorted into a Scrooge, a blue-nosed witch hunter, a sadistic and cruel father, a man filled with greedy fevers, hateful tempers, and raging anger. There are many who have considered the matter carefully who would agree that it is this supposedly respectable teaching about the nature of man that did the real damage. One effect was to make such a mockery of marriage and the sanctity of vows which Christians had been able to keep for centuries that the laws became unenforceable. Even the Episcopal Church had to rewrite its ancient canon governing marriage in order to try to accommodate to the actual conditions with which we were faced. Perhaps those of you who are acquainted with James Mitchell's discussion of the new marriage canon[5] were struck, as I was, with the discovery that it was based on the novel assumption that marriage was not a union under God, but a status established by human law which might be altered by a church council. Once again the mythical beast called the state, the being that has no being and yet frightens men to death, had moved into the place of God. Since the ruler of the state is always a man, under the new system it was a man moving into the place of God—which is St. Paul's description of the anti-Christ. Marriage was so commonly recognized as a legal institution, established by law and maintained by law, that the real purpose of law to support *God's* demands was abandoned even by the Episcopal Church.

I cannot remember having heard of a policeman being called to arrest a known adulterer: it is always the divorce attorney. What the law supposedly has made, the law taketh away. The only trouble is that the system has led to appallingly careless marriages, a trail of wrecked hopes and homes, a general weakening of the entire social order, and a further willingness to let the state somehow pick up the pieces. Today we even ask the state to pay unwed mothers so much per illegitimate child. Present conditions are but a hair's breadth from the ultimate socialist dream, a community of wives. Perhaps that sounds so far fetched as to be ignored. But that is exactly what the all-powerful Mao Tse Tung, a man sitting in the place of God and calling himself the state, is doing in China. That is exactly what Adolph Hitler tried to do in his night of terror in Germany. Ancient Sparta tried to adapt the scheme as outlined in Plato, and the signs are not absent in our own midst. I have heard Joseph Fletcher, a professor at the Episcopal Theological School in Cambridge, Massachusetts, declare publicly that there is nothing in group marriage that is contrary to Christian doctrine.

We must also take very seriously the mantle of respectability which has been cast over such outrages to marital responsibility and fidelity as birth control, artificial insemination and much so-called marriage counseling that concentrates on sexual satisfaction. The participation in talks on these matters by churchmen of all denominations who make a display of their church affiliation is not without effect. Marriage is becoming commonly approached as a legal solution to a biological inconvenience.

All this is but spade work for sowing the dragon's teeth in welfare laws that make it a responsibility of the state to pay unwed mothers for raising bastards. I will leave it to social workers to detail what is happening to those people who receive such payments. The abuses are notorious. But the description of the fact is unnecessary. Anyone can see in a moment what the child support laws accomplish. Motherhood is a biological misfortune, responsibility for which is shared, not by a husband forced by

---

[5] An unpublished study by James B. Mitchell, McAlester, Oklahoma.

law to fulfill his marriage vows, but by the state. The law assumes that a marriage and a family is not the necessary social unit for nurture of the young, only that the state, for whom the children were begotten anyway, see to it the bills are paid. By some odd quirk, mothers are accepted as the best possible agents of the state to teach and train the young: no questions are asked about the rather obvious disqualifications involved in illegitimacy. Any difficulties in enforcing the law against adultery is avoided by the simple expedient of doing away with marriage. Without marriage there is no such thing as adultery, and no law against it. The state is then forced into the role of regulating instead of punishing. By assuming financial support of the children, it regulates their nurture, involves itself in the morals of mothers, encourages illicit "affairs" extending over many years and in general steps into what is commonly thought of as that area in which each individual is most supremely and personally responsible for himself. How men can delude themselves into thinking the state really can regulate things connected with the breeding of children is hard to imagine. It is more astonishing than the practice of idolatry in the eyes Isaiah who heaped scorn on men for worshipping the stock of a tree which they used to fulfill their needs. Yet it is apparent that as enforcement of the law against adultery fades away, payment of child support to unwed mothers fill the vacuum. Regulation replaces punishment.

EIGHTH COMMANDMENT

Thou shalt not steal.

THIS commandment, like most of the others, sets up a legal guarantee of what we sometimes call the natural rights of man. The first four, to be sure, give legal support to what we might call the inherent rights of God among men, and the fifth recognizes God's chain of command through father and mother. Beginning with the sixth, "Thou shalt do no murder," we have the legal foundation for the concept so firm in the minds of the Founding Fathers of our government: the right of every man to life, liberty, and property. The function of the law is to inflict punishment and vengeance upon any man who presumes to take away from another any of these things. The familiar phrase from the United States Declaration of Independence—life, liberty, and the pursuit of happiness— was and is a recognized exception to the far more common and correct, "life, liberty, and property."

All the writers and thinkers who inspired the early Americans agreed with the universal Christian value upon private property. Their reasoning behind the emphasis upon the right of property as inherent in the nature of man need not concern us here. It is enough to recognize it. It is important, also, to understand what part the law can and does play in securing these rights. It was never supposed that the law was the source of them. Neither the Constitution, nor the Declaration of Independence, nor the common law nor any positive law nor even the law of God gives man these rights. They are simply distinctive properties of human nature, without which a being is no longer human: "All men are endowed by their Creator with certain inalienable rights." The basic "right" involved is the right to be a man. There is a strong Christian line of thought which makes most of us restless with the talk about "rights" even in that sense; natural man, says one theologian, has no rights. Be that as it may, man has, as man, a mission upon earth. He is to exercise dominion over it. We have seen that it is to preserve this created order, with man ruling the earth, that God requires man to avenge the blood of man. On the same principle of authority man's liberty must be inviolate. He cannot exercise authority without it. His liberty is supremely expressed in this power to give or withhold freely his consent to another person in what we call marriage. That consent, once given, must be guaranteed in Heaven and thus liberty is preserved by punishment for adultery. Finally, man's property must remain inviolate if he is to have dominion over material things. Man, to be a man, must have life, liberty and property. In that sense he has "rights." In a more important sense, each of us, inheriting and sharing the heavy weight of glory, is bound to avenge any attack upon humanity. Man must do the avenging in order to restore a disrupted order. Any act of rebellion in the form of a violation of any of these basic "rights" must be put down by a man, or manhood has been dethroned.

Finally, it is important to see that the quality of manhood is completed in every individual man. The race as a whole, or the mass man, is no more manhood than every individual person. Associations, partnerships or corporations have no powers or properties except those derived from their individual members and which exist in each of the members. Thus the "right" of humanity to own property is expressed in what we call "private property"—the power of every individual human being to exercise ownership (complete control) over creatures and material things. If any individual is stripped of his mysterious power of ownership, manhood itself is desecrated just as effectively as in Adam's fall, or in an act of murder. It is well known that responsibility cannot be delegated; and individuals cannot delegate their responsibility for their own things to others, not even to the state. In the mystery of the market, ownership is made lively and liberty a reality. Anyone who steals a man's property instead of trading for it or begging has violated human dominion as surely as a murderer; and vengeance must be taken upon him by a man. The law requires such vengeance and in that sense protects these "rights."

Thus it is a crime for any man or group of men to steal anything from another. Furthermore, it doesn't take much pondering to realize that the power of ownership must be absolute. It is black or white; I own a thing or I don't. I may own part of it, but there is no such thing as a part of ownership. Christians have a commonplace saying that every man's home is his castle. He is king in his own residence; he may go to any lengths to stop a trespass; soldiers, in the United States, may not be quartered in his home without his consent; and not even a policeman may enter without a proper warrant issued under careful safeguards. If a man really owns his property, he may refuse to sell it, even to a king, as Naboth refused to sell his vineyard to King Ahab. He may dispose of it at his death by will; he may develop it or not as he sees fit, and within the limits of it there isn't much he can't do. The same conditions apply to personal property and money.

Today there seems to be an almost uncontrollable urge on the part of some people to say a man has control over his own property as long as he doesn't infringe upon the rights of his neighbor. Let me point out that the proviso is irrelevant. To say a man has control over what is his own gives him no rights over what belongs to somebody else. No man, of course, may use his own property in order to exercise control over another's. Such acts, however, are adequately covered in the other commandments. The only real infringements on the rights and properties of others are covered by the laws against murder, adultery, thievery, false witness, and covetousness.

Also the extent of my obligation to keep up my property in order to increase the value of my neighbor's is indeed a questionable one. If the condition of my property per se affects the value of his, then I have an interest in his, his right of ownership is dissolved, and nobody has anything to be stolen. The concept abroad today of *common* ownership is not a new idea or one that Christian people have never considered before. I suppose every generation toys with the idea in one way or another. What we call "common ownership," however, is in reality merely the extension of the right of private property to certain organized bodies. A congregation, for example, has common ownership of certain properties. Yet no one for a moment would think that by it the private rights of ownership are abrogated. We have merely set up an organization to which we entrust all rights of ownership for things which we use in common for certain purposes. The vestry of an Episcopal congregation has full authority over that property and is accountable to the congregation for its election to office. Actual control of the *use* of the property is vested in one man—the rector. Ownership is thus temporarily vested in whoever happens to be holding particular office at a given time; but ownership remains fixed. It adheres to whatever individual is properly designated.

By our common ownership of church property, we in no way give up our private rights to own other property. In fact, we may say our common or joint ownership depends upon our individual powers. That such reasoning is fully in accord with that of the church in the Book of Acts is abundantly clear. Much has been made of the statement in one place that the church people "held all things in common."[1] Some people have pointed to that passage and declared that the early church thus attempted communism. However, joint ownership is not communism, and Peter said expressly that Ananias and Sapphira, who were struck dead for *lying* about the price they received for their land, were punished for *lying*, not for withholding part of the money. Peter never questioned their power to do as they pleased with either the money or the land.

What we call communism is not common ownership, but the stripping of any kind of ownership from all men and vesting it only in the hands of the head of the government. The matter was thoroughly explored and even experimented with way back in the days of Henry VIII and Elizabeth I. It was attempted as pilot projects involved in the deep ferment of the Reformation and was rejected all around. Under Elizabeth the matter was expressly decided and incorporated in the Articles of Religion which were approved and adopted by the Episcopal Church and are printed in the back of the Book of Common Prayer. There, in Article 38, it reads: "The Riches and Goods of Christians are not common, as touching the right, title and possession of the same; as certain Anabaptists do falsely boast." The article then goes on to state once again a privilege and responsibility of ownership—to give some away as well as to keep some or sell some. It continues: "Notwithstanding, every man ought, of such

---

[1] Acts 4:32 ff.

95

things as he possesseth, liberally to give alms to the poor, according to his ability." Again, what I don't own, I can't give away. The more we explore the matter, the more incontestable appears the right of private property, and the more essential the burden upon governments to punish severely anyone who interferes.

Yet the very fact that I have had to make a rather lengthy apology for sacredness of private property is evidence of the widespread attack upon it. That it is fully recognized in our law should be readily admitted. It remains to show how liberal forces would abolish individual powers and vest all "ownership" in that mythical beast called the state. To those who grant the Hegelian principle, inherent in all socialism, that the state is god walking upon earth and has absolute rights of immediate ownership of all the earth, such private rights as men may be allowed are understood to be held at the sufferance of the state. The extraneous question of whether the man with official powers is a wiser administrator than a private person is always introduced to support the claim that his bureaucratic superior wisdom entitles him to ownership. Because of the supposed superior wisdom inherent in official status, ownership is in fact abolished and humanity debased before an idol.

Under God's law, the government may sometimes be ceded the power to force the sale of a piece of property which may be deemed necessary to it to accomplish its mission of common defense. That uneasy cession is granted in the United States as the right of eminent domain. It is hedged around with careful safeguards which supposedly prevent the government from any act of seizure or plunder. (A forced sale is but a gentle kind of seizure!) Nevertheless, jury trial is required, and sufficient cause must be demonstrated, so that private rights seem to be adequately observed. Yet even that right is often questioned in Christian lands, and governments are denied certain properties, even in time of war. (Although it is true they often go ahead and seize what they need to carry on a war, such an act is either frankly banditry, or is pretended to be a trumped-up criminal offense.) David did not consider he had any right to seize, or even take as a gift, a threshing floor upon which to build an altar in the interests of the health and welfare of the whole nation. Fortunately the owner was prepared either to sell or give away his property. We may presume David would have had to go elsewhere if he had not. Ahab couldn't force Naboth to sell his vineyard; and even Joseph had to buy up the land of the Egyptians in time of famine in order to get title for Pharaoh. Christian governments exist to punish severely anyone who tries to steal anything from another. Yet today we commonly accept the idea that the government can not only force the sale of a man's home to build a road, but that it actually owns and disposes of all the property in a great city through the machinery of "Urban Renewal." Eminent domain has been stretched to allow the United States government to seize the good low farmland of the Tennessee Valley, flood it, and capture the water of the whole area to be divided through a sluice gate according to decree. So-called reclaimed land is the poor highland country. Where outright ownership is not seized, regulations, such as those in zoning codes, are imposed that in effect abolish all private right and responsibility. Railroads may not charge prices except those the government allows; oil companies may produce only what the railroad commission permits. And, under the rationing scheme, no one could buy or sell without government license.

The conditions fit all too nearly the description in St. John's vision of the reign of the anti-Christ: "No man might buy or sell, save he that had the mark, or the name of the beast, or the number of his name."[2] During World War II nobody could buy or sell without a ration card and stamps. Surely rationing was a rehearsal for the final end. The income tax, which seizes property under pain of the most severe punishment, virtually abolishes any man's control over what is his own, and substitutes full government regulation over all life for just punishment of crime. The state, which is supposed to punish thieves, becomes itself a monster thief. It plunders men's property as Robin Hood did in order to distribute it according to the ideas of the man who happens to be running the show at the moment. The law, which exists to limit stealing, becomes the instrument by which ruthless men seize all property, from the greatest factory to the widow's loaf of bread. A man's house is transformed from his castle to his burden which may be taken from him by any wild dreamer who proposes a plan for what he calls civic betterment. The poor who might get a toe-hold in the opportunities of the city by living in cheap tenements are denied the chance by slum clearance projects. The rich must hire a battery of experts to advise them as to how to keep out of jail in the management of their affairs. A man is accountable to the government for how he uses whatever he thinks he owns, but at any moment the government may rob him of it.

All this is done in the name of justice. It is Robin Hood's justice, in which the rich are robbed and the poor share in the loot. That keeps the poor off the robber's back and stops the crowd from attacking him. Whom else would anyone rob but the rich? I know of no better discussion of the subject than the work of a French economist, statesman, and author who published a little book in 1850 called *The Law*. The author is Frederic Bastiat. As long ago as 1850, two years after Karl Marx published his Manifesto, when the socialist evil was boiling and stewing all over Europe, Bastiat analyzed the problem in terms of the law against stealing. Even at that time the process advocated by the socialists was easy to follow.

He wrote: "Unfortunately, law by no means confines itself to its proper functions. And when it has exceeded its proper functions, it has not done

---

[2] Rev. 13:17

so merely in some inconsequential and debatable matters. The law has gone further than this; it has acted in direct opposition to its own purpose. The law has been used to destroy its own objective: it has been applied to annihilating the justice that it was supposed to maintain; to limiting and destroying rights which its real purpose was to respect. The law has placed the collective force at the disposal of the unscrupulous who wish, without risk, to exploit the person, liberty, and property of others. It has converted plunder into a right, in order to protect plunder. And it has converted lawful defense into a crime, in order to punish lawful defense.

"How has this perversion of the law been accomplished? And what have been the results?

"The law has been perverted by the influence of two entirely different causes: stupid greed and false philanthropy."[3]

Long ago Jesus warned that the Gentiles are ruled by those who are called benefactors, or do-gooders. "It shall not be so among you," he said. Stupid greed and false philanthropy are two sides of the same coin. Liberality is a great privilege, a blessing of great possessions: truly it is more blessed to give than to receive. Men who are greedy for the power inherent in giving away much goods are the men we call do-gooders. Unfortunately, the effect of such actions on both the law and society is disastrous.

To quote Bastiat further: "No society can exist unless the laws are respected to a certain degree . . . When law and morality contradict each other, the citizen has the cruel alternative of either losing his moral sense or losing his respect for the law. These two evils are of equal consequence, and it would be difficult for a person to choose between them. The nature of the law is to maintain justice. This is so much the case that, in the minds of the people, law and justice are one and the same thing. There is in all of us a strong disposition to believe that anything lawful is also legitimate. This belief is so widespread that many persons have erroneously held that things are 'just' because law makes them so. Thus, in order to make plunder appear just and sacred to many consciences, it is only necessary for the law to decree and sanction it. Slavery, restrictions, and monopoly find defenders not only among those who profit from them but also among those who suffer from them."[4]

Now someone will say, "Well, one hundred years ago Bastiat was worried about the same things we are; so things can't be so bad." But wait. He saw the same end to the matter. But you and I are living much closer to the end. Our conditions are vastly changed. In his day the process was only started. He foretold what was to come—things that are now part of the accepted order. He said: ". . . imagine that this fatal principle (of lawful

---

[3] Bastiat, Frederick, *The Law*, The Foundation for Economic Education, Inc., Irvington-on-Hudson, New York, 1950. Page 8.
[4] Ibid, Page 12.

plunder) has been introduced: under the pretense of organization, regulation, protection, or encouragement, the law takes property from one person and gives it to another; the law takes the wealth of all and gives it to a few—whether farmers, manufacturers, shipowners, artists, or comedians. Under these circumstances, then certainly every class will aspire to grasp the law, and logically so. The excluded classes will furiously demand their right to vote—and will overthrow society rather than not to obtain it."[5]

That was over one hundred years ago. In my own lifetime Lloyd George led the English workers in a great ballot revolt. Slogans were used which quite frankly regarded the newly granted ballot as a weapon to achieve plunder. In 1960 we witnessed a debasing campaign which pandered frankly to the lust for plunder in order to elect a President of the United States: the dominant issue was an insulting appeal to the nation's lowest class of voters with promises of shares in the loot. As Bastiat observes, the principle is the same in every age. If the "robber barons" of the last century were entitled to use the law to plunder the property of others, so are racial minorities, illiterates, juveniles, and vagabonds today. It all depends on who gets his hands on the machinery of the law. But God's law applies alike to king and beggar. Military power and collective force offer no exemption from the law of the Father of Jesus Christ. His law shall not be broken, for God is not mocked. The penalty, if not inflicted by men, will come in the form of a terrible judgment of God Himself upon the whole race. The law stands in all its rigorous purity, demanding vengeance for every desecration of man by any creature.

---

[5] Ibid, Page 17.

NINTH COMMANDMENT

Thou shalt not bear false witness against thy neighbor.

THE Ninth Commandment is the first to make mention of a man's neighbor. Nevertheless, it is "thy neighbor" who is covered by the Second Table of the Law—the last six commandments upholding the crown of humanity. It seems almost a truism to say that no one can break any of these laws except against the person nigh him, who is his neighbor. The traditional summary of the law, quoted by Jesus as covering the entire Second Table with the commandment, "Thou shalt love thy neighbor as thyself," makes plain sense. Yet a tremendous effort has been made for decades to reduce the law to nonsense and make it of none effect by redefining "neighbor." We are taught from the cradle on that our real neighbors are the people farthest away from us. That is supposed to be so because of jet planes. Children are taught they must love their "world neighbors," or "neighbors in Africa," with shameful disregard of the fact that such "neighbors" are of necessity imaginary and unreal and answer to idolatry. The real task in life is to accept the dignity and humanity of persons whose independence and dignity are impressed upon us, often uncomfortably, simply by their near presence. The first law of the Second Table commands honor to the nearest persons we know, father and mother, to be superseded only by one still nearer—husband or wife.

Here we discuss the crime of making a false accusation against another person, who must also be near since normally no other accusation would be entertained at all. Perhaps in this connection I should deal with the verse from Genesis which is so often thrown into any discussion of law and order. That is the smart-alec quip which Cain blurted out in defiance of his Creator after he murdered his brother. God asked Cain a perfectly natural question, which as far as Cain was concerned might or might not have been prompted by His knowledge of the murder. God said, "Where is Abel thy brother?" But Cain, smeared with guilt, snarled in reply, "Am I my brother's keeper?" God does not answer that question. It deserved to be ignored. Clearly he is not his brother's keeper. But Cain betrayed himself by asking it. It is one thing to be your brother's keeper, and to deprive him of responsibility for himself, and to be his master, and to have him your slave. It is another thing to murder him, or steal from him, or accuse him falsely of a crime so that he will be destroyed. Cain tried to cover up his criminal action by raising the question of slavery and independence. Nowhere in Scripture do I find Cain's rhetorical question answered in the affirmative—yes, you are your brother's keeper. In fact, the answer is quite the opposite. The Psalmist sings:

"But no man may deliver his brother, nor give a ransom unto God for him.

"For it cost more to redeem their souls, so that he must let that alone forever."[1]

---

[1] Psalm 49:7, Prayer Book version (Coverdale).

103

It is one thing to assume responsibility for my brother's welfare. It is something else again to refrain from telling a lie about him to the judge. The Ninth Commandment simply makes it a crime to accuse him falsely. The matter, again, is integral to the whole operation of law and justice. There can be no action at the bar apart from the determination of the fact in question. And the determination of any fact depends upon the witness of a human being. The only way to determine that something happened is that a witness appear who will testify to his own personal knowledge of it. The only way to bring about the punishment of a criminal is for some person to bear witness of his personal knowledge that the crime was committed by the accused.

Legal machinery among the people of Israel put a burden upon every adult male to participate in the execution of justice. The witness, by virtue of the unique information he possessed, became a public official, personally responsible to initiate the trial and, upon conviction, to cast the first stone in the execution. Among us this terrible responsibility is once removed in the sense that we delegate the responsibility to certain officials to push the matter. Nevertheless, the public prosecutor even for us is merely the agent of the person who is the witness. It is the witness to a crime who holds the key to whether the criminal will be punished. He, too, is a public officer by virtue of what he has seen and heard.

I think it should be emphasized that no man can testify *except* to what he himself has seen or heard. I am a witness only to that of which I have personal knowledge. I may repeat the witness of another, for I am witness to his witness: but not to the fact. Quite as clearly there is a powerful temptation to abuse or confuse the function of witness for any of a number of reasons. Children learn quickly that by tale-bearing they can get another child into trouble: it is so easy to get big brother spanked by telling on him. It is just a short step to tell something only guessed at, but not seen or heard. The commonly accepted principle of morality, apart from legal practice, is illustrated by a story about Abraham Lincoln. It seems that the charge that Mr. Lincoln was an infidel was freely made in his campaign for Congress against Peter Cartwright, whom he defeated. Mr. Lincoln replied to the charge with a letter to the editor in which he said in part: "Mr. Woodward . . . may have *believed* what he said; but there is, even in that charitable view of his case, one lesson in morals which he might, not without profit, learn of even me—and that is, never to add the weight of his character to a charge against his fellow man, without *knowing* it to be true.—I believe it is an established maxim in morals that he who makes an assertion without knowing whether it is true or false, is guilty of falsehood; and the accidental truth of the assertion, does not justify or excuse him."[2]

---

[2] Jones, Edgar DeWitt, *Lincoln and the Preachers*, Harper, New York, 1959, Page 137.

The law must hold every witness accountable. Otherwise the courts would become instruments of grudges, fears, hatred and weaknesses. Courts would be agents of violence and chaos, not orderly process, if they could not punish severely any departure from absolute honesty and precision by any witness. The usual procedure is that set forth in Deuteronomy: *"If the witness be a false witness, and hath testified falsely against his brother: then shall ye do unto him, as he had thought to have done unto his brother: so shalt thou put the evil away from among you."*[3]

There have been times and places among Christians, as in sixteenth century Geneva, when it was common practice for the accuser to be jailed at the same time as the accused. One of them was guilty. In this connection it is worth quoting an appeal made by the heretic Michael Servetus from prison, not to recall the issues aroused by that affair, but to point to the evidently common practice of the law. He wrote to the Geneva Council, "Gentlemen, I demand that my false accuser, John Calvin, [false only according to Servetus] be punished with the *lex talionis* and be detained prisoner as I myself until the case be finished by the death of one or the other of us, or some other punishment. And for this purpose I formally indict him with the said punishment of the *lex talionis*. I am content to die if he is not convicted, either of this or of other things which I shall bring against him."[4] It is interesting to note that Servetus admits his own guilt of false witness by saying he knows he can show his opponent is guilty of something, if not of false witness; also that Servetus' real accuser, a man who spotted him at church, one Nicolas de la Fontaine, was imprisoned at the moment of the heretic's arrest.

The law and the principle stand in Texas and the rest of the United States. Every person under Christian law has recourse in both criminal and civil courts against false arrest. We have that recourse even against policemen. Our police officers are not empowered to make arbitrary arrests. They may act only upon their own witness to apprehend a criminal, or upon information solemnly sworn to in a warrant. Any person, official or not, who gives false testimony causing arrest is severely dealt with. I am told by the district attorney's office that in Texas there are only eight crimes for which the death penalty may be assigned: one of these is the bearing of false witness in a trial in which the death penalty is returned. *"Ye shall do unto him, as he had thought to have done unto his brother,"* is the law in Texas, too.

Those enemies of God's law today who try to abolish the death penalty for murder on the grounds that it is possible to have a miscarriage of justice would do well to consider the whole law which would exact the death penalty upon anyone responsible for that miscarriage. Obviously

---

[3] Deuteronomy 19:18-19.
[4] Cadier, Jean, *The Man God Mastered,* Inter-varsity Fellowship, London, English Edition, 1960, Page 160.

there cannot be any such miscarriage apart from a false witness. Certainly the matter is of deadly seriousness. But the argument that murder should not be punished because some men might be liars is absurd. Two wrongs cannot make a right. It is only necessary to enforce rigidly the whole law. It is those who would openly seek to abolish the whole law of God with whom we are concerned here.

If God's law is not our law, then we have no choice but to submit to a regulatory state which is what men mean by a totalitarian tyranny. A state that does enforce the Ten Commandments would punish its own officials who tried to arrogate to themselves God's powers to make laws and to regulate life. It would then be God's minister, testifying to His power and glory. The only way the state can escape thus serving God is that it not enforce God's laws. That means it must impose a whole new system of law which looks to the control of every detail of the lives of its subjects since it cannot punish crime. And, just as there is only one way to build an arch, there is only one way to build a government not under God, the Father of our Lord Jesus Christ. That is the way of the anti-Christ. The government of the anti-Christ is characterized by three key features: it requires its head, a man, to be worshipped as god; it accomplishes amazing mechanical and scientific signs and wonders to bedazzle the minds of men; and it regulates the market. False witnesses are not enemies of the anti-Christ and they go unpunished in his realm as do murderers, thieves and adulterers. They are rather "corrected" and taught to commit their evil deeds in a kindly manner. The kindly manner seems to have something to do with loving thy neighbor against whom one has falsely informed, or whose goods one has seized, or whose life one has taken.

The alternative is no idle fear. It is the actual procedure of every socialist tyranny we have seen, from the Soviet to Castro's Cuba. There is no more vivid picture of the national socialist terror of Germany, or the international socialist terror of Soviet Russia, than that of hob-nailed boots at the door in the night. We read too much to doubt the reality of the Storm Trooper who knocks at the door to seize a member of the household and carry him off into oblivion without any charge being made, any witnesses produced, any conviction determined. Informing is a necessary part of the machinery of a totalitarian government; and informing cannot proceed if the rules of true witness are observed.

We are told repeatedly, in Cuba as elsewhere, that the first thing that happens after a revolutionist takes over is the blood bath turned on by informers. Men are encouraged to inform against their neighbors—gossip, hearsay, guesswork, anything that might give a hint of defection or lack of zeal for the new regime is devoured hungrily. Those informed against have no recourse, no protection. They usually have become enemies of the state, if they were not already so, by virtue of their false arrest. Therefore,

106

they must be done away with as a preventive measure. No action need be taken by such a government against the informer because he, by virtue of his guilt, is psychologically committed to continue his informing and to betray all persons—father and mother, friends, children, and neighbors—to ingratiate himself with the state. Surely it is an indescribable horror for a government, whose mission it is to exact vengeance upon a false witness, to foster and encourage false witness instead. Yet I cannot see how it is possible for a government which does not severely punish a false witness to avoid encouraging him. The welfare state must do so in the normal course of its regulatory procedure; and, if nothing else, human carelessness inclines every one of us so that we need restraint against wild guesses and strong statements which amount to false witness without necessary intentional malice to start with. And I see no reason to suppose intentional malice has disappeared among us.

Here I am sure it is necessary to mention the question of communist sympathizers. Many people are said to be such; others raise a hue and cry as though to say so were to bear false witness. However, let me observe that as far as I know to accuse a person of sympathizing with communism is not to accuse him of a crime. Moreover, the accusation is subject to determination: that is, it can be demonstrated that a person did openly sympathize with the aims and methods of communism. The truth or falsity of the witness is subject to determination, and, if damage is done falsely to the accused, there is plenty of recourse under this law. I find no shrinking horror among many men, clergymen as well as others, openly to express sympathy with what they themselves call communism. I find no reason to doubt the general reliability of what these men say as being what they mean; and I find no reason to suppose they do not understand what they are saying and therefore no reason not to call them communist sympathizers. Otherwise, no man could be held accountable for what he says. Also, it is a specific count to state: "So-and-so was identified by such-and-such in a published sheet as being associated with an organization which itself has been identified by so-and-so as a communist front." That is a statement of personal knowledge and determinable fact. If the published information is false, there is plenty of recourse against the publishers.

And in this connection let me observe that if the most horrible sort of accusation we can imagine is to accuse a person of being a communist sympathizer, then think how horrible a thing it must bt to sympathize in any way with communism. Sympathizers who resent being called sympathizers are in fact expressing condemnation of themselves which is not necessarily implied in a plain statement of fact. And I think I must add another observation: revulsion against an evil does not insure freedom from it. Those sins we commit are usually the ones we most abhor. There is a jingle that goes something like this:

The sins we are most inclined to
Are those we've most a mind to
see in others.

There is another facet of false witness in the area of slander and libel. Clearly, damaging witness can be borne and is borne against people without benefit of law courts. To make a public accusation, either by spoken word or by written word, is often almost as deadly to a man's good name and his life and liberty as false arrest. And so it is a crime among us not only to swear out a false warrant, but even to publish false accusations. I don't suppose any group of persons is more conscious of the libel laws than newspaper reporters who every day have the sword of judgment hanging over their heads. I can assure you libel laws are real; they are effective; and they are enforced. Rare is the man who will not seize an opportunity, or even the obligation, to clear his name against a matter of public record in which he is falsely accused. Curiously enough, the one unshakable defense against libel and slander, I am told, is the truth of the statement at issue. Truth is our defense against false witness, slander, and libel. We are perfectly entitled to assume the truth of any serious public accusation which is not challenged by the victim under the laws of slander and libel.

Also I believe we are all free to make of the truth what deductions and evaluations we choose. That is, having determined what is true, I have the personal liberty to think what I choose about what it means. To deny any man that liberty of evaluation of the import of a truth is to deny the whole fabric of liberty of conscience.

While the Ninth Commandment remains intact in the criminal code of most of the United States, it is not only ignored in the vast operation of administrative law of the burgeoning welfare state, but is aggressively defied. The agencies of the government that administer various welfare programs must have access to protected informers in order to function. An informer in the administrative system merely furnishes rumors, tips and accusations upon which investigators may begin to hound their prey. Since guilt under administrative law is not the proof of commission of a crime against God, but a slip in the performance of routine activities, the victim must prove his innocence and he cannot tell what constitutes innocence. The truth or falsehood of the informer's accusation is not important: it merely opens the case for probing. He is useless if he must account for the truth or falsity of his witness. Not only that, but his very identity must be kept secret, or he is liable to private reprisals from his victims after they have been finished with by the hungry bureaucrats, and he is not so willing to furnish tips to keep the investigators going.

One of the most familiar regulations to Americans is that governing the examination of income tax reports. Under authority of Congress, the Bureau of Internal Revenue has decreed in regulations effective in 1961 how informers are to be used and protected by all the power of the United States government: "A district director may approve such reward as he deems suitable for information that leads to the detection and punishment of any person guilty of violating any internal revenue law, or conniving at the same." After giving much detail about how the reward shall be paid, the regulations state further that "No unauthorized person shall be advised of the identity of an informant." The only authorized persons are those connected with paying the reward or pursuing the investigation.

That the informant system is inherent in a government that is engaged in regulating life instead of punishing crime is clear from the experience of Great Britain in the case of the Milk Board Tribunals. These special courts were set up in 1932 to police the laws regulating the distribution of milk. According to George Widner, formerly a solicitor of the Supreme Court of New Zealand writing in *The Freeman,* a British lawyer was horrified when he witnessed a trial before one of these tribunals. He saw the accused pronounced guilty and heavily fined *on the hearsay evidence of the board's own servants.* Mr. Widner reports responsible opinion to the effect that the head of a welfare department "is in England subject to a merely formal legal control, and is beyond all effective judicial supervision."[5] In other words, the accused has no case to bring against anyone who might bear false witness against him, and no court to which he can plead for redress.

The bearing of all this on careless name calling in public pronouncements is painfully evident. Men of purpose and conviction have never been slow to call a spade a spade, or a liar a liar. But they were doing so under the terrible and awesome knowledge that if one man calls another a liar, one of them is one. And it never paid to be the one. Men who used bold language were prepared to answer for what they said, and did not retreat with a smile behind loud protestations of love, refusing to come out and answer for their slanders. By the same token, people who are apt to be called to account for false witness and for slander and libel usually begin to discover the difference between a real slander and the merely horrified raising of the eyebrow with, "Him? My deah . . . after all . . . not him." Such display of condemnation would call for an explanation: and it is unlikely anybody would be impressed to discover that such a one was "controversial." After all, wherever Jesus went among men, there was a division because of Him. Even so, they could not find witnesses who could agree in their testimony against Him and He had to be condemned illegally— the testimony of His own mouth in answer to the high priest. The council itself became witness to His claim to be the Christ, and thus acted as both prosecutor and judge.

Surely no man was ever condemned as immoral by Christians on the

[5] *The Freeman,* August, 1957.

vague charge of using "methods." The late Senator McCarthy was roundly condemned for "his methods." But the characteristic of his methods, the identifying aspect, was that they were his. They may or may not have been attractive: but it is hard to understand how they could be subject for an accusation by a witness responsible before God, the law and the general public.

As the public sensitivity wanes, and administrative law replaces regular judicial processes, the way is speedily prepared for the bully inquisitor who knows no restraint and operates with the full terror of untrammeled force of government.

TENTH COMMANDMENT

Thou shalt not covet thy neighbor's house, thou shalt not covet thy neighbor's wife, nor his manservant, nor his maidservant, nor his ox, nor his ass, nor anything that is thy neighbor's.

THIS commandment touches upon the root of all crime. Perhaps for that reason it is so often spread so thin as virtually to lose all real meaning. In one sense it forbids an attitude, or a frame of mind, out of which come violations of all other commandments. For example, one steals if he covets another man's property. One murders if he covets the life of another. He curses father or mother if he covets the honor which belongs to them. St. Paul sees the full cup of covetousness in idolatry because in that vile practice a man takes to himself worship that belongs only to God. True as all this may be, it is odd indeed to find a law which forbids a frame of mind, or a mental attitude.

I cannot help recalling a comic strip of Mutt and Jeff many years ago in this connection. Mutt and Jeff were playing big league baseball. Jeff was the umpire; Mutt was up to bat. Jeff warned him that any vile language or abuse of the umpire would get him thrown out of the game. At the next pitched ball, he called a wild strike. Mutt said nary a word, just looked at Jeff. Jeff threw him out of the game. When Mutt protested that he hadn't said a word, Jeff said, "No, but oh, what you were thinking!" Now that's funny in a comic strip. But in law enforcement such procedure is hair-raising. Yet in classroom discussions in seminary and in weighty tomes of the scholars, I have met much serious speculation on what the government should do about what somebody supposedly is thinking.

Lawyers who deal with the necessity at times to prove intent on the part of a criminal to commit a crime know the difficulties involved. Indeed, apart from a subsequent action reasonably unexplainable except for mental predisposition, it probably is impossible. That is, if a man has stolen, we may presume he intended to. But if he has done nothing, how can there be any evidence that a person intended to? Even if he tells you—is that enough to punish him? I would say not. He probably had not real intent—only a passing notion. And so, quite naturally, if the Tenth Commandment is interpreted as dealing with a mental attitude, it loses all force as law. Perhaps it is for this reason that the Tenth Commandment is subject to such wide and varied misuse, while real criminal violations of it are rampant and go undetected, to say nothing of going unpunished.

In the official teaching of the Roman and Lutheran Churches, for example, the Tenth Commandment is separated into two commandments instead of one. That compensates for combining the First and Second into one. Two crimes, or rather sinful mental attitudes, are then analyzed. One, set apart as the Ninth Commandment, has to do with lasciviousness, being limited to the phrase, "thou shalt not covet thy neighbor's wife." The other has to do with avarice, or greed, as drawn from the prohibition against coveting thy neighbor's goods and property. Certainly we would agree that lasciviousness and avarice are vicious and sinful mental attitudes,

113

or moral failures. But I cannot see how they are crimes. A man who commits adultery is undoubtedly lascivious: but there is no crime, no broken law, no penalty to be assigned, until he has done the deed, and his crime is taking for himself what belongs to another. A man who steals, or murders, or worships idols is undoubtedly wracked with avarice; but there is no crime until he has taken something which is not his own. And so the commandment, being interpreted as a prohibition against personal spiritual disease, becomes meaningless as a law forbidding a specific crime.

Again, this commandment has sometimes been so broadly interpreted as to become silly. I have seen it written that mention of the wife as something that might be coveted shows a society in which women are regarded as chattel. Such a society is then adjudged as undeveloped and at least partly savage, and it follows that the whole law becomes questionable for this modern enlightened age. Now I can see no reason to suppose for a moment that a man's wife must be thought of as an unfeeling, impersonal bit of property in order to be the object of somebody's covetousness. Neither do I see any reason to suppose that an imagined state of equality of the sexes has in any way altered the fact that it is impossible for a woman to overpower and force a man. Therefore, "covet thy neighbor's husband" is likely to be a futile gesture.

To clear up the matter we must give careful attention to what the Bible says: no more, and no less. First of all, the word "covet," while it expresses an attitude that is dangerous, does not describe something which of itself is bad. "To covet" simply means to have an inordinate desire for something. It is dangerous because we mortals are so prone to desire the wrong thing. But the Bible speaks of the time that the Children of Israel coveted food—and with no disparagement. And St. Paul writes that we should "covet earnestly the best gifts" of the Spirit. Moreover, the Tenth Commandment is explicit. It does not say simply, "Thou shalt not covet." It says, "Thou shalt not covet . . . anything that is thy neighbor's." It does not legislate against envy. It does not forbid a desire to keep up with the Joneses. It does not say, "Thou shalt not covet a hat *like* Mrs. Jones', or an automobile *like* his." It says you must not want Mrs. Jones' hat, or his car. Therein lies a world of difference—the difference between a crime and a bad disposition.

If the only way to get possession of what belongs to somebody else were by direct personal action, such as stealing, or murder, or adultery, I suppose there would be no need for this last law. But just as the forces of law can be used to punish wickedness, they also can be misused to accomplish wickedness. The classic example is the case of the two harlots who came to Solomon each claiming the same baby as her own. One party to the dispute had to be making a claim to what belonged to the other.

Just as some people are prone to use the force of government to harm an enemy by bearing false witness against him, so some people would use the force of government to seize another man's property by entering a false claim to a rightful share. Both actions are themselves criminal. The steps may be outlined:

1. The covetous person asserts a claim.

2. The rightful owner clings to his own.

3. The false claimant cannot now back down so appeals in righteous indignation to the court who has police power to seize the goods in dispute.

4. Proof of ownership cannot be offered, so the judge makes a division between the litigants.

5. The true owner demurs, often preferring to give up all rather than see the property ruined. (The good shepherd will die for the sheep because they are his own.)

6. The covetous person cries, "Unfair" and says, "Destroy the property; if I can't have it, nobody else can." He poses as noble and righteous, concerned only for "justice" and not things.

---

1. The harlot whose son had died said to the other, "The living is my son."

2. The other harlot replied, "No; but the dead is thy son, and the living is my son."

3. "Then came there two women, that were harlots, unto the king, and stood before him."

4. "And the king said, Divide the living child in two, and give half to the one, and half to the other."

5. "Then spake the woman whose the living child was unto the king, . . . and she said, O my lord, give her the living child, and in no wise slay it."

6. "But the other said, Let it be neither mine nor thine, but divide it."

An even more penetrating illustration was the response of Jesus in the case of the young man who cried out for him to make his brother divide the inheritance with him. Jesus replied, "Beware of covetousness." When two people claim possession or ownership of the same thing, clearly one of them is acting in covetousness: he covets what belongs to his neighbor. If the false claim can be determined and exposed, the guilty person is subject to counter action and heavy penalties.

However, a covetous action need not always come to court, as it did between the two women before Solomon. One can win public consent to a false claim by talking loudly enough and long enough and menacingly enough to force a surrender of ownership. It is the character of the ungodly, from the days of the Psalm writers, that they prevail with their tongues. They shout down all opposition, they seize all means of public communication, they take the floor in a debate and won't give up. They beat down any rightful opposition by a mere torrent of words spewing forth from twisted mouths and roaring printing presses.

"The piece of land you thought was yours is *my* land."

"The cattle you have rounded up are *my* cattle."

"The factory you thought you owned is *my* factory."

"The privilege of citizenship which you have is *my* privilege."

"The responsibility for making family decisions is not the husband's and father's but *mine,* the wife's, or the whole family's through something called the democratic process."

"The responsibility you thought you had for your own well-being is not yours but *mine,* which I will enforce upon you by government."

Such wild claims are sufficiently familiar that I need only mention them to substantiate them.

Men often covet another's power or position even more than his goods. A statement by the late suave and witty bully of the socialist cause, George Bernard Shaw, is worth repeating. On the last page of *The Intelligent Woman's Guide to Socialism,* according to a Veritas publication,[1] Shaw declares: ". . . under Socialism you would not be allowed to be poor. You would be forcibly fed, clothed, lodged, taught, and employed whether you liked it or not. If it were discovered that you had not character and industry enough to be worth all this trouble, you might possibly be executed in a kindly manner; but whilst you were permitted to live you would have to live well." Shaw here openly runs the gamut of evil— fully as violent and fully as vicious as Adolph Hitler—assuming his own right, through something mysteriously called *Socialism,* to ownership, body and soul, of every living human. In the crime of coveting every man's God-given control and responsibility for himself (and consequently all that is his own) a man plunges into the depth of depravity which would establish government regulation of all things. He would force you to eat, to be clothed, to be confined behind walls, to be taught, and to be employed, according to his own conscious will. Such a condition in moderation is called slavery. Forced feeding and drinking has generally been thought to be impossible. I don't know what to make of forced teaching, or forced education, or forced love of other persons.

Strangely enough, the suburbs of Hell and the beginnings of wickedness are those we seem likely to get most excited over. Taxi drivers in New York will rage and fume at each other over who has a right to carry a passenger; but they will not bat an eye at the union organizer who takes from them their control over their own taxis and jobs. Farmers will kill their neighbors over irrigation water rights, but the same men will sit by idly while the

---

[1] *Keynes at Harvard,* Veritas Foundation, 1960, Page 32.

government strips them of any right to plant or harvest their own crops. Parents will burst into a rage at a teacher who presumes to spank their child; but day after day, year after year, they will take that child to a school over which they have no control, let him be subjected to a teaching that begins by ruling out any mention of Jesus Christ, and give up their inherent responsibility for that child's training. Businessmen will guard jealously their sales contracts and yet not turn a hair when they lose all control over their employees. Citizens of the United States will quarrel with their neighbors to the point of breaking a friendship over an election and never consider that the war-making power of the United States, which belongs to Congress and the President, is coveted by the State Department for an as yet non-existent world government.

The covetous actions of the ungodly today have reached far beyond the outskirts of ownership and control of things, or the authority over employees, or the allegiance of a wife. No facet of covetousness is overlooked or omitted in the amazing claims of the socialists. The goal is so daring it is breathtaking. The collectivist is so sweeping in his claims he leaves his opposition stunned. Shaw, for example, does not stop at claiming a right to your house. He simply sets up a mythical creature called the state— a creature fully under his control since it exists only in his imagination— and avers with an air of unruffled authority that you don't own anything: the state owns everything. The state, say he and all socialists, has the last word on everything, thus destroying all meaning to ownership or dominion. It is said to be wrong and immoral for any being except the state to own anything. The state owns all property. The state is also said to own your children: they are not yours, after all, but the state's. The state also owns your mind. You thought it was yours, that you could believe what your conscience directed. But no, it is in the interests of the state that your mind be trained to respond to certain impulses and to give back certain indoctrination. The state owns your house, too. You may pay for the repairs, of course, but the state will decide how many feet you may put it from the street, what sort of material you must use, what you may and may not do inside of it. And finally, if it chooses, the state may tear it down and put an apartment house or a freeway there.

You thought at least you had ownership and control over your own choice of friends and associates. But, wait. Not so fast. It is the state that must decide these things. The state, which is said to be responsible for training your children (always remembering there is some person running the state), is also making it perfectly plain that you have no control over the associations of your child in school. It matters not what is important to you. The very queer little thing you hold important is the thing the state has singled out to violate, thus making sure you feel the weight of your chains. Or perhaps you think you retain control over your own decision to buy or sell. But try it. The state has precluded you. It has what are called "fair trade" laws, confiscating goods from the merchants if they decide to move their goods below a certain price set by the state. In other words, some person or persons, by manipulating the machinery of the state, has coveted the money with which you generally make a bargain and has robbed you of any value in that money apart from his approval.

Perhaps the most obvious and choice maneuver, however, has been to organize for covetous purposes. No one would seriously maintain that an employee, by mere virtue of his employment, owns a share of a business. But by organizing all the employees, or some of them, into a disciplined corps that threatens violence, men can coerce employers to give certain rights of ownership to the head of the union. From terms of employment, the union inevitably proceeds to the management of the business and claims its right to run the whole thing. All this is done with the support and often advice of the government, which even supervises union elections, thus giving the unions a legitimate status under law.

The grim final twist, then, is that the union, while supposing it is using the government's force to seize the employer's powers of ownership and management, winds up itself under enslavement of the very governmental force it sought to manipulate. The government, established to punish criminals, having itself become a party to the crime of coveting, resorts to full regulation. When it forces a man to pay certain wages and work certain hours, it must also use its force to regulate prices, stifle competition, stipulate production and allocate markets. By failing to serve properly to punish crime, the state degenerates into a tyrannous regulator.

Covetousness, which I have said is often seen as the root of all crime, is so rampant among us, so commonly put up with, and so universally operative that whatever legal protection there may be in this country is seldom resorted to any more. The condition of itself would be bad enough. But there is one further aspect of all covetousness to consider. There is a universal mark of the covetous person. Like the false mother before Solomon, he says, "Let it be neither mine nor thine, but divide it."[2] If I can't have what belongs to somebody else, destroy it. For someone else to have what I have not is "unfair." If I can't be rich, then divide the wealth, share it, wipe it out. If I can't have a first-class education, then divide it, water it down, destroy it, and don't let anybody have it. If I can't raise a good crop of cotton and make a good year, then divide the entire crop and don't let anybody make it. Justice is perverted from equal enforcement of punishment to redistribution of wealth.

Terrifyingly, the covetous person can never be satisfied. His lust cannot help turning to a passion to kill and destroy. For no matter what Solomon ruled, the false mother could never make herself the real one. Even had

---

[2] I Kings 3:26.

118

she been awarded the whole child, her covetous passions would have filled her with murderous rage over the frustration of the fact that the child was not hers and could never be made hers. So the covetous manipulators of powers of the state: they can never get control of my mind. It will think what I make it think as long as it exists, no matter what hours I may be forced to spend in class, no matter what gobbledegook I may be compelled to read and repeat. It remains mine, and the covetous person can only, at last, in a fury of blind rage, destroy me. So with my farm and my house. No matter how many rules and regulations may be imposed, no matter how frantically the covetous men may pursue my thoughts and actions, there remains an area of independence which they are physically incapable of ruling. They always know these things do not in truth belong either to the state or to them: ownership is not answerable to that kind of control. So they must resort to destruction.

The covetous men must tear down my house to put up a park; they must cover my farm with water in order to have a fishing resort; they must take my child out of my family at birth and put him into a commune; they must start by making the age younger and younger for nursery school; they must show their absurd control over the steel industry to the point they ruin it. So mass organized covetousness moves inevitably to mass organized slaughter. Let the world be neither God's nor mine, but divide it—kill it—destroy it. How foolish of us to imagine that such people walk about in a rage, have long scraggly beards and bloodshot eyes, lurking in dark corners and butting heads over cellar tables dimly lit by candle. It was George Bernard Shaw who openly advocated that spirit of the destroyer—Shaw the brilliant, Shaw the witty, Shaw the genteel, Shaw the man of the university, the theater, and the lecture hall. Those who insist on controlling what is their own, including their own immortal souls, will, wrote Shaw, "be executed in a kindly manner." In America it was Stuart Chase, whose books were used as the last word in guides to style for English composition when I was an undergraduate student, who wrote, "The sixteen methods of becoming wealthy would be prescribed (under the system he was advocating) by firing squad if necessary." "Thus," comments the Veritas writer, "the 'gentle socialists' would enforce their Keynesian formulas."[3]

Covetousness is ultimately expressed in seeking control over thy neighbor's own person, having already coveted his family and his goods. The state, using the force of the community to seize goods and persons, must become absolute ruler, a totalitarian tyranny, answering to the New Testament description of the anti-Christ who causes himself to be worshipped above all that is called god. He violates God's law, and substitutes his own powers of regulation by force of arms.

---

[3] *Keynes at Harvard*, Page 79.

CONCLUSION

The foregoing analysis of the structure of Christian society in the United States under the law of God should make clear the nature of the only alternative structure toward which man could strive. The Christian order, which requires punishment for violation of laws that are given by God, rests upon the realization that God, the law-giver, has total power. If the Christian system is to be replaced with a new structure, there must be a new and different law-giver who hands down other laws and to whom must be attributed the authority which is God's. The problem, then, for those who would restructure the social order with the socialists, is first of all to establish a new ruler sitting in the place where God ought to be. We may dismiss the possibility of another god, and we are left with what turns out to be the only real scheme, which is to elevate man to total authority. In the words of the socialist writer Martin Buber, the objective is to erect a new order of society in which "everything is subordinated to conscious human will, indeed . . . designed as though there were no other factors at work."[1]

The socialist may grapple endlessly with the problem of what kind of structure will be produced by conscious human will, but it is patently impossible to erect any kind of order until human will is established as supreme authority. Thus all socialism and any other alternative to the Christian order of society must be dedicated exclusively to setting up complete regulatory powers in government. The power of a human agency to regulate every aspect of human life, extending even to the thoughts of men, becomes of necessity the description of any social order other than Christian. The Biblical portrayal of the final achievement of the anti-Christ is accurately met by the avowed utopian passion of the socialist to enthrone man in the place of Christ.

The structure or order of society is defined and maintained by its system of law. That is not to say that the law equals society; but it is to say that the social order is supported and exists by the enforcement of its laws. Clearly it is necessary in order that the social order may stand at all that the laws must apply equally to all men. Judgment must be rendered without respect of persons, and the punishment must fit the crime, not the criminal. It is a mark of human dignity that every member of society knows better than to break the laws, and every member holds personal responsibility for his own obedience. Each individual, moreover, shares full personal responsibility not only for obedience but also for enforcement. The framework in which he lives cannot stand, and his own existence would thereby be thrown in jeopardy, if not ended, if the laws can be broken with impunity. When laws are broken and no punishment follows,

[1] Supra.

there is no law. Such is the description of anarchy or chaos which we may recognize as an unbearable state of existence.

The close association of justice and equality is understandable as long as the law is God's law and criminals are those who have violated a clearly defined moral order established by the Creator Himself, and equality means an equal application of punishment. When the law is twisted to replace God with conscious human will, then justice must be renamed. It is called *social* justice, and equality becomes twisted to mean equal possession of all things from authority to this world's goods. Equality before the law is an end that can be realized. It is sensible, and all men respond to it. Equality in the social sense, however, is an absurdity which men have long since understood is approachable only in total slavery and is reached only in death.

Individual Christian moral obligation clearly, then, extends far beyond mere obedience to the law: it includes responsibility for enforcement. One of the charges which God is pictured as bringing against His people in the Day of Judgment is precisely that they rejected the responsibility for law enforcement. "When thou sawest a thief, then thou consentedst with him."[2] The picture is a vivid one. It is easy to imagine seeing a burglar break into a jewelry store and rob it. The person thus seeing the crime who fails to raise the cry, "Stop, thief!" is guilty equally with the thief himself. The awful judgment of St. Luke upon Saul, the persecuting Pharisee, is contained in the simple statement that when Stephen was stoned to death, "Saul was consenting."[3] The burden of responsibility for law enforcement is not limited to the established officials. These act only as special agents. Every individual in Christian society becomes a public official with a weighty responsibility for law enforcement by mere virtue of the fact that he has personal knowledge of a crime. As witness he bears public responsibility for prosecution. The public prosecutor provides technical advice and service. Punishment is a responsibility that ultimately falls on individual members of a Christian society. In Israel the responsibility was expressed by the means of stoning a criminal to death. Each individual thus took a direct hand in executing punishment. The same principle is expressed in Christian society through public punishments, including public executions. The process involves the mystery of common guilt, and it is inconceivable that such a process would fail in its purpose. Those who participate in the punishment do not present themselves as faultless, but accept the guilt and remedy it by withdrawing their consent to the crime. It is interesting in this connection to observe that one of the most forceful arguments advanced by liberals who would abolish capital punishment is that the present practice of near-secret executions fails utterly, even to serve as a warning to others.

[2] Psalm 50:18.
[3] Acts 8:1.

The burden of law enforcement is far heavier than the burden of obedience. Every parent knows how he must screw up his will to spank a child. It takes very little imagination indeed for a person to realize the moral courage that would be demanded of him to make an arrest personally. Even if he can imagine crying, "Stop, thief!" he comes near to breaking out in a cold sweat simply thinking about physically apprehending the thief all by himself. Yet if he fails, he has consented with the thief and is equally culpable with him. He has subordinated himself to the power of the thief and is governed by the man and by human power to do him hurt rather than by the law of God.

The realization of the great importance of consent throws responsibility for tyrannical government squarely upon the shoulders of its subjects. A tyrant could not begin to achieve total power unless the public generally consented to numberless criminal acts which he has committed. It is no mere coincidence that men like Castro, Stalin and Khrushchev arrive in power upon a great pile of wrecked laws, having themselves stolen other men's property, murdered men, committed adultery, borne false witness, sworn falsely, and generally made havoc of the Ten Commandments. Had they been punished for the first of their crimes, they would not be alive to enslave millions. Their power is granted by the consent of millions who prefer to submit to them rather than risk the danger inherent in effecting punishment. It is sobering indeed to realize that God will not hold him guiltless who has consented with the thief. We who submit to the tyrant must answer before the Throne of Heaven for the very crimes the tyrant has committed. We will not be able to plead an excuse for our own unrighteous acts in obedience to the tyrant's will on the grounds that we were unable to resist him. We will rather suffer the wrath of God for our failure to resist.

The Christian community certainly exists as the church to forgive sins. It cannot, however, forgive an unrepentant sinner. That would make a mockery of righteousness. He must be dealt with by a Christian magistrate, who is God's minister for wrath. A broken law can be repaired by penitence as well as by punishment. But penitence must not be confused with public consent to crime. It is easy to see that socialism would soon vanish from public conversation if the Christian people of the world were obedient to the law of God to the extent that they refused even to consent with the law breakers.